The Wildwoods Dad

By Don Oakland

Oak Press
904 Broadway Ave.
Wausau, WI 54401

Copyright © 1990 by Don Oakland
FIRST PRINTING 1987
SECOND PRINTING 1990

All rights reserved. No part of this book may be reproduced or transmitted in any form or by any means, electronic or mechanical, including photocopying, recording, or by an information storage and retrieval system, without permission in writing from the publisher.

ISBN 0-9615242-1-9

Published by:
Oak Press
904 Broadway Ave., Wausau, WI 54401

Distributed by:
Adventure Publications
P.O. 269
Cambridge, MN 55008

1-800-678-7006

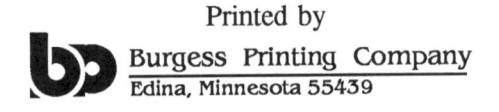

Printed by
Burgess Printing Company
Edina, Minnesota 55439

This book is dedicated to my daughters, Sarah and Melissa. I hope when they become old enough to read, they will have developed a forgiving sense of humor. I'd also like to thank Cynthia Schley for again lending her artistic talent to this project. Special thanks to Belinda Brame, Tera Schleicher and my wife, Kathy, for helping me proofread the battered prose. Thanks to John Froelich for capturing a rare moment on film--my kids sitting still for more than a second; to Leon Tietyen for printing the photograph, and to Paul Jaeger for his support.

This book was written on a Macintosh 512K Enhanced computer using Microsoft Works software. Camera ready materials were produced by using Microsoft Word 3.0 software on a Macintosh Plus computer to convert Works text to Palatino 12 point type reduced 10 percent. Final pages were produced on an Apple Laserwriter Plus. Special thanks to Team Electronics, Schofield, and Ironwood Press, Winona, for their assistance.

Table of Contents

Chapter 1	Outdoor Ordeals................................1
Chapter 2	Chaos and Kids.............................. 35
Chapter 3	Parenthood and Other Hazards.........59
Chapter 4	Society Slightly Askew......................93
Chapter 5	Life on the Loose............................123
Chapter 6	Household Horrors..........................159
Chapter 7	Whacky Work Stories......................193
Chapter 8	Weird Santa Saga...........................217

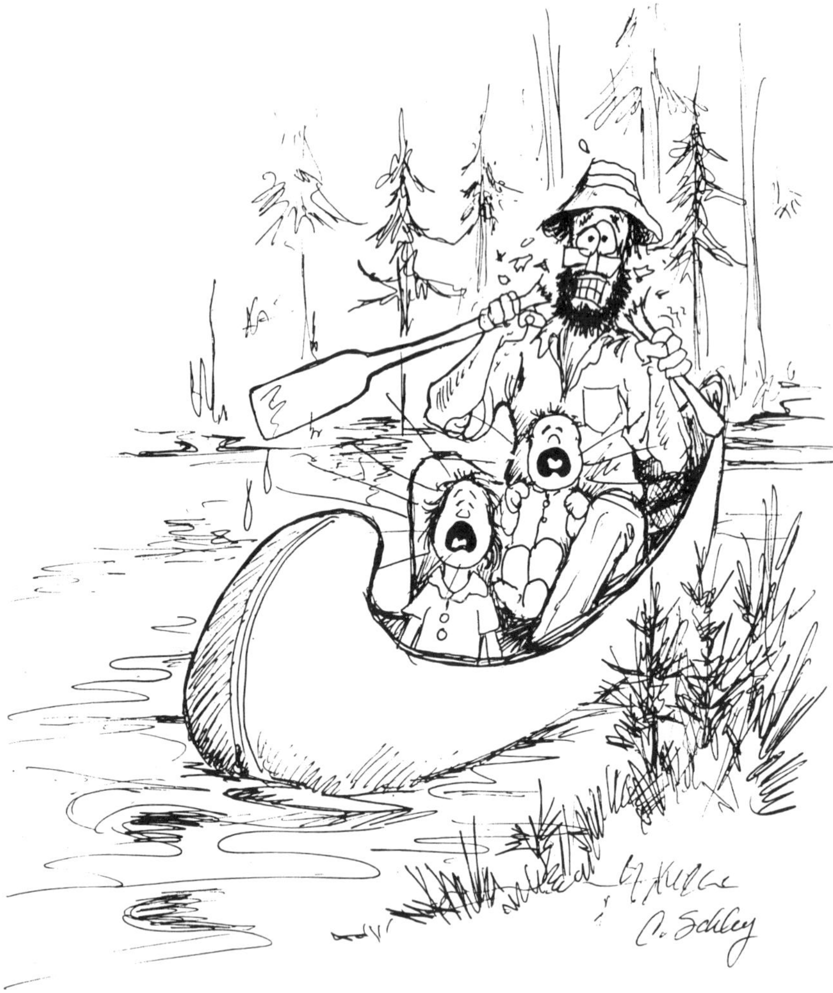

Chapter I

Why I run to the wildwoods

Why am I a wildwoods man?

Why do I leave the comforts of home and the convenience of the city to wander about the woods or roll along in a canoe on the gentle waves of a isolated lake so small it is but a dot on the map.

Why do I get up, put on wet socks and frozen boots and spend most of the day dragging a canoe up a rain starved river?

Why?

Is it that I love the birds and bees and can name every tree in the forest?

Is it that I seek the biggest buck or the wiliest of fish?

Is it I come from a proud heritage of pioneers, mountaineers and trappers?

Why?

The answer is simple. My wife and kids drive me there, that's why.

A hundred miles from the nearest town, deep in some woods surrounded by swamp so thick moose fear to tread, I find a valuable treasure. Peace and quiet.

That's all I ask of the great outdoors. Peace and quiet.

I'll gladly trade frost frozen boots for dirty diapers.

I'd rather portage a heavy canoe and a week's worth of supplies over roughest of terrain than be awakened in the middle of the night to the sound of a baby with an ear infection crying her lungs out.

I'll eagerly eat half cooked oatmeal and pancakes without syrup if given the chance to eat a meal without yelling at the kids to clean their plates or pick up the banana that was abruptly thrown to the floor.

I'll gladly spend an afternoon on a lake and not get one bite just to be rid of bills and arguments over family finances.

Why do I seek out the wildwoods?

I tell you why. Telephones.

The best thing about the wilderness is AT&T is not among its inhabitants. You don't find pay phones attached to every corner tree.

Birds singing replace telephones ringing.

Nobody comes by my tent, rips open the flap and says, "Oakland it's for you!"

Watches.

There are no watches in the woods, at least not on my arm.

The last thing I do before leaving civilization is to take off my watch. It is sort of a symbolic act.

No longer is my life governed by little red digits.

Morning is when the sun comes up (or the old men of the group get up). Noon is when breakfast wears off. Supper is whenever somebody gets ambitious enough to build a fire. Bedtime is A) when the fire dies or B) after the second glass of whiskey is finished.

Everything is reduced to its simpliest form.

You cook because you are hungry, not because the clock says if you don't eat now you'll miss the six o'clock news.

You sleep because you are tired.

When you work, you work hard. And, when you rest it is without guilt.

The comforts are reduced to well-hydrated food, dry toilet paper, a warm chamois shirt and a cushion on the canoe seat.

The woods is an peaceful island amid a raging sea of over-civilized civilization.

Fair weather trip yields no tall tales

It is a real bummer coming back from Canada without any good stories to tell. If you go into the wilderness with only a pack on your back and a 17-foot aluminum canoe dragging behind you to somehow test your manliness against the elements, you should come back from such an endeavor with something other than mosquito bites on the back of your legs.

You should come back with tales of adversity which cause the mouths of those listening to drop open in awe.

Well, this year my trip to Canada produced no such tales.

Who wants to hear that the weather was good, that the fish didn't bite well or that the food was tasty and satisfying?

I'd much rather sit down with my desk-bound friends and weave stories of woodland agony climaxed by a thrilling account of a near heroic landing of a monsterous fish.

But, this year all I can talk about is the mosquitoes which came out on all those sunny days we experienced.

In previous years I told about half-mile portages down trails so narrow that they were hardly distinguishable from deer trails, and so steep they made Rib Mountain look tame.

I could recount how I set up my tent in a driving rain well after dusk. The only thing that kept me going was the hope that I would soon be dry inside the nylon structure. But, when I finally got in, I discovered the bottom of the tent felt like a wet towel and that the sack holding my sleeping bag had leaked.

But, this year everything stayed dry. It didn't even rain the first day, a rarity during our early fall trips.

In previous years I could make you groan with stories of how we dragged fully loaded canoes up and over beaver dams four feet high and how we struggled over raging rapids swirling about sharp boulders.

But, this year the water was deeper. The beaver dams were absent, probably washed away by some downpour weeks earlier. The higher water also buried many of those sharp rocks which were like can openers against the hulls of our canoes.

Every visit to Canada has produced at least one good fish story. Like last year when my brother-in-law inadvertently hooked a northern that looked as big as a crocodile with teeth to match. Somehow he got the darn thing into the canoe, a narrow vessel holding myself and a young lad who had never seen anything larger than a perch before.

Suddenly the fish ripped the line from its mouth and thrashed freely in the bottom of the boat. I swear, the kid was ready to abandon ship. Without a net in the canoe, I figured my only recourse was to take the paddle in my hand and whack the bugger upside the head. I stood up and swung that paddle like Reggie Jackson's bat. Unfortunately, I missed the fish and nearly knocked my brother-in-law overboard.

Meanwhile the fish summoned all its strength, flipped itself high into the air and over the edge of the canoe.

This year produced some good sized northern and trout, but nothing to write home to mother about.

About the only thing I can talk about as I scratch the back of my legs, is how I slept with worms one night.

We could tell by the clear night sky that the next morning would bring a frost that would probably spell curtains for the nightcrawlers I was packing.

So that night I put the cottage cheese container holding the worms in the bottom of my sleeping bag.

I'm happy to report the worms survived. But, boy, did I have weird dreams that night.

The Captain thinks bigger is better

Often an outdoor writer is forced to exaggerate certain events in order to achieve a certain level of dramatic effect. In the preceding story, I mentioned a certain fishing event which occurred during one of my many trips into the Canadian wilderness.

Realizing my editors would be less than impressed with such a mundane fishing story, I decided to enhance the story in roughly the same manner as a fisherman enhances the size of his catch with a wide-angle camera lens.

I assured my editors the tale was factual, or at least based on fact. I mean, a fisherman should be allowed a little latitude in recounting the events which led up to his catch or the valiant struggle which tragically ended with an empty net.

So here is the official version of the story about the Canadian northern which got away. I personally believe it is far more readable than the "factual" account.

Editor's Note: This is an outdoor epic about one man's quest for a legendary fish which lives in a lake in Canada. We offer this with apologies to the spirit of Herman Melville...

Little did I know what I was getting myself into when I signed up for a Canadian fishing trip with "The Captain."

I had been told we would be fishing for brook trout and walleye, yet here was this man, the leader of our expedition, dashing about a Wausau tackle shop buying huge lures.

"Aye, lad, the bigger the lure, the bigger the fish," he told me as he ripped a huge silver spoon off the wall rack. "If it doesn't cost more than a $1 an inch, it isn't any darn good."

He grabbed a spool of 20-pound test line and gave me a wicked look that made me uneasy inside.

"The man gets lure lust every fishing trip," one of the crew told me the next day as we packed our gear into the back of a Ford pickup.

"He doesn't pack enough warm clothes because he needs the space for his fishing tackle," the crew member said in a hushed voice. "Darn pack of his weighs a ton. Boy, never, ever, ask to carry it."

Through the night we traveled. By morning we were weaving through the granite bluffs of southern Ontario. The captain was sitting next to me in the truck.

"Aye, lad, it was five years ago that I saw that a-cursed fish," he grumbled.

"Say what," I asked half asleep.

"We were in a canoe drifting along the lakeshore. My partner threw out a spoon and started to reel 'er in. Suddenly beneath the surface of the water appeared this huge shadow. It was the biggest northern I'd ever seen.

"Ever since that day I have vowed to catch that demon fish," he said as that wicked look returned to his eyes.

An hour later our four canoes were crossing a pristine Ontario lake toward a questionable destiny. We portaged over a heavily forested hill to a mile-long lake which had been reduced to a pond of floating muck by someone who years earlier had dynamited a beaver dam.

It was a hostile land. Canadian fishing guides did everything they could to keep their lakes inaccessible. Yet, nothing they did could stop the captain.

Just after guides would assure their clients the lake was theirs and only theirs, the captain would paddle through. He'd yell out that his canoes were from the Holiday Inn on the other side of the ridge.

We paddled on through the stagnant water bubbling with methane and hydrogen sulfate gas. It was like one big liquid landfill.

One guy lit up a cigarette; blew his canoe right out of the water.

After the muck pond came another mile-long portage.

A normal crew would have rested or even turned back. But the captain drove us on for another unmerciful five hours.

The next day we reached our base camp, a small clearing on the shore of a wilderness lake. Somewhere out there, hiding in a deep hole, was an awesome fish, a fish with a tail as big as a paddle blade.

That evening the men sat around the campfire dickering over who would carry the captain's canoe on the upcoming portages. Because it weighed twice as much as the other canoes, they called it "The Gunboat."

Men would sell their wives to avoid carrying it. But, an offer to carry the canoe in exchange for the Buck knife on one's belt, would be met with an angry "No Way!" A broken back is a small price to pay for a good knife.

The captain didn't sit by the campfire, but stood by the shore. He stared at the dark waters of the lake and the star filled sky above.

Suddenly a meteor streaked across the southern horizon.

"A sign!" the captain yelled as he stretched his arms toward the heavens. "Tomorrow, he shall be ours."

I looked down at my supper. It resembled library paste soaked with red dye.

The cook said it was chili. The crew had their doubts.

But, no one complained.

One year a brash young man complained to the cook that you could pave a driveway with the chicken-rice casserole he had made.

That night the cook hung several dead fish by the young man's tent. After that big black bear got through with that young fellow, he looked worse than the casserole.

Most of the men killed the aftertaste of supper with whiskey.

With this crew, a flask of whiskey or rum was required gear.

"Whiskey is a great liniment," the captain told me as he downed his second shot. "It's the only one that works from the inside out."

The men were particularly fond of a drink they called Twang, a mixture of Tang orange drink and a hefty dose of 151 proof rum. It quickly wiped from memory the day's hard paddling while providing a daily dose of vitamin C.

The following day the men paddled across the lake in search of trout and walleye. Within hours they had their limits.

But the captain wasn't impressed. To him there was only one fish worth catching.

Suddenly the captain's eyes widened and he abruptly stood up in the canoe.

"Behold! The birds! To your paddles, men, for he is a-rising!" he yelled.

"Uh, sir, that's only a seagull," I said meekly.

"Blast you, man, paddle! We have little time!" he said grabbing his fishing pole.

As we approached a small weed bed, the captain cast his lure. Suddenly his rod bent like a willow stick.

The fish began pulling our canoe like a powerboat towing a skier across the lake.

"The net, man! Get the NET!" the captain screamed as he frantically cranked on the reel.

I grabbed the net, looked over the edge of the canoe and came face to face with the biggest northern I'd ever seen. I quickly scooped the big fish into the boat.

In an instant the fish was out of the net and thrashing about. With one mighty twist, he yanked the lure from his mouth.

"Grab him, boy!" the captain yelled.

"You gotta be kidding!" I screamed back. "He'd take my hand off!"

The captain stood up, grabbed a paddle and brought it down like an ax toward the fish. The paddle missed the fish and slammed into the bottom of the canoe. The impact caused a small leak to appear. He tried again and missed again.

The canoe started rocking violently. The next thing I remember was the canoe flipping out from under my legs and the sharp chill of the lake water against my face. I recall looking up and seeing the captain and the fish entangled in monofilament line. A treble hook dangled from the captain's nose and a steel leader was wedged between two of his front teeth.

That was the last anyone ever saw of the fish or the captain

When the rest of the crew found me, I was clinging to a worm bucket floating among the weeds.

So, be warned, dear fisherman. If you go up to Canada, you may hook into a big fish... or the devil himself.

Mountain peak was not the only thing bare

I always wondered what it would be like to stand on top of a mountain.

But, I never figured that when that opportunity came I'd find a half naked girl up there.

I expected a beautiful view, not a beautiful girl skinny dipping in a crystal clear, snowcap cold, mountain lake.

Women's lib had reached new heights.

When my wife suggested we attend a family reunion in Colorado, I agreed to go on the condition that I be allowed to escape from the family gatherings long enough to climb a mountain, any mountain.

In Wisconsin we don't have mountains, real mountains. There's Rib Mountain, but by Colorado standards it amounts to a mere foothill.

"Just as the country boy yearns to visit the city, I'm a flatlander yearning to be a mountain man, if only for a few hours," I told my wife.

My wife replied with one of her Donald-don't-be-silly looks and resumed doing the dishes.

Thank goodness her dad was more enthusiastic. Born and raised in the Colorado Rockies, he was as eager as I was to venture into the high country.

Why the first thing he did when we arrived in Glenwood Springs was to show me a mountain.

"That's Mount Sopris. Is it mountain enough for you?"

"How tall is it," I asked as I stared at the snowcapped peak high above the Roaring Fork River Valley.

"About 13,000."

"Wow."

The highest I'd ever been was good ol' Rib which stands all of 1,942 feet. I began wondering if I had bit off more than I could climb.

The night before our climb, my wife's dad and all his Colorado relation spent the better part of the evening telling me about all the dangers of mountain climbing.

"The air is so thin up there you'll lose your breath, get dizzy and maybe die," one said.

"Don't go off the trails. Heard of men who got so lost they have yet to be found," said another.

"Weather can change in an instant. One minute it's sun shiny and warm, and the next it's a blinding blizzard."

"But, it's summer," I interjected.

"Boy, the mountains have their own seasons. You can have a foot of snow on the Fourth of July."

My wife overheard the conversation and told her dad he'd better not let me get lost because no way was she going to singlehandedly chase after our two kids for the rest of the trip.

The first thing I learned about mountains is that they appear closer than they are. When we got out of the car, I figured an hour's walk and we'd be at timberline. Three hours later I was still walking through aspen woods.

The second thing I learned is that trails leading up to mountains are steep and less than smooth. My feet began aching from walking over the rock strewn trail.

About noon we reached a small lake at the foot of the timberline. There was nothing between the lake and the peak but a billion rocks. Except for the steep slope, the peak looked surprisingly close, maybe a half mile at most, I figured.

My father-in-law stayed behind as my brother-in-law and I continued on. There was no trail, just rock piled on top of rock. Crossing them was like walking across a field of teetertotters.

A half an hour passed and the peak looked no closer than it did from the lake. And, even though we were walking-crawling most of the way, I began feeling like I had just run a mile or two.

We quit our ascent when we discovered what had appeared like a slope from the lake was actually a sheer cliff a hundred or so feet high. We could see a way around it, but time was running out. And, the clouds seemed to be getting thicker.

We returned to the mountain lake and sat down to enjoy its snow cold water. I'd never tasted water so good.

I was lifting my head from the water when I looked up and saw three guys and a girl standing on the opposite shore. They obviously saw us, but that didn't seem to bother them.

Then to my amazement they began undressing. The next thing I knew the gal was wearing nothing but her panties and was wading into the lake.

"Quick, get your camera," my brother-in-law said nudging me in the ribs.

"What, are you crazy! There's three of them and two of us and anyway, how'd I explain the picture to my wife!"

Well, the gal was out of the water in about 30 seconds. Heck, I couldn't keep my hand in it for more than a few seconds, it was that cold.

11

The girl got dressed and the four of them disappeared into the woods.

Later when we caught up with my father-in-law, I remarked how much I admired the wildlife which came to visit the lakes of the timberline.

Why being lazy is unsafe

One of the biggest mistakes a person canoeing through the wildwoods can make is being lazy.

I know, I've been there.

Oh, I didn't call it being lazy. No, I called it being efficient. My intentions were purely noble...to save my canoeing companion and me time and energy.

I mean, is trying to avoid a portage being lazy?

Yet, every time I try an alternative to carrying a canoe cross country, I get into trouble.

Take for instance beaver dams.

There are three ways to get a canoe over a beaver dam.

You can unload your canoe and portage around them.

You can paddle up to the dam, parallel park your canoe next to the stick and stone structure and lift the canoe over.

Or, if you are upstream from the beaver dam, you can paddle like mad and try to plow through or over it.

I have yet to portage around a beaver dam.

Many times my brother-in-law and I have lifted fully loaded canoes over the dams. Although relatively efficient, the operation usually results in one of us getting wet up to the knees.

The third option has worked sometimes, sometimes not.

Like the time my brother-in-law paddled furiously toward this big beaver dam. We were going like the

University of Wisconsin rowing team when the bow hit the beaver barrier. Unfortunately, that's where the bow stopped and my brother-in-law began his flight.

It was quite a sight watching my brother-in-law, two packs, three rods and a seat cushion crash into the water 10 yards downstream.

Another time we attacked a beaver dam with similar passion and ended up high centered on the mass of logs and sticks. As the canoe sat like a giant teetertotter, I could hear the fiberglass hull of the canoe snap and crack.

When my brother-in-law got out, the bow of the canoe shot up and I did a half somersault into the deep end of the beaver pond.

The other problem wilderness canoers face is rapids.

Now, I'm not much of a whitewater man, but if it means avoiding a portage, I'll risk it.

There are two ways to navigate rapids. You can either walk the canoe through them or paddle through the jigsaw puzzle of rock and whitewater.

Walking through rapids is a guaranteed bath.

It never fails that my feet find that super-slippery rock or that bottomless deep hole.

Once I got my boot wedged between two rocks and spent a half an hour in waist deep water trying to free myself while trying to keep the canoe from taking a fast trip downstream.

A couple of years ago, I felt brave and chose to run a small rapids which ended in a two foot drop.

"It's a straight shot," I told my sternman.

It was indeed a straight shot. And, we navigated it beautifully. However, I neglected to calculate the weight of the canoe and the angle it assumed as it went over the falls. I realized my error as I watched the bow disappear under a haystack wave and a wall of water hit my lap and fill the canoe with three inches of river.

The guys in the canoe behind us tried the same thing and capsized. Yet, their gear ended up being drier than ours.

Laziness tends to cloud your judgment. You forget where your abilities as a paddler end.

"Sure we can get through there," I told my brother-in-law as we looked over a 100 yard long rock garden. "All we have to do is bear to the left. Why, I bet we won't hit one rock."

"I don't know, it looks awfully fast," he said cautiously.

"Look, either we run the rapids or spend the next hour and a half hiking gear through thick woods."

"Well, all right," he said as he paddled the bow toward the edge of the fast water.

Soon the canoe was zipping along like some log ride at an amusement park. It was exhilarating until my brother-in-law spotted that big boulder in our path.

"Right!" he yelled.

"What?"

"Look out!"

The next thing I knew the canoe was high centered on a big round boulder. All forward motion stopped and we found ourselves turning like some huge propeller.

"Do something!" I cried.

"Like what?"

Well, I never got around to answering him because at that instant, the current had lifted the canoe off the rock. Unfortunately, we were facing backwards at the time.

Ever try to paddle a canoe backwards?

Before we could turn around, the canoe had hit four or five rocks and was quickly turning perpendicular to the current.

"PADDLE!" my brother-in-law yelled.

I rammed my paddle into the foaming waters, but instead of finding water, my paddle blade found rock. The paddle snapped out of my hands and within moments was floating 15 feet ahead of us.

"PADDLE!"

"WITH WHAT!" I screamed as I held up my paddleless hands.

"Oh, lord!"

Well, for the next few minutes the canoe bounced its way down the rapids like a steel ball in a pinball machine. Amazingly the canoe on its own navigated the rapids better than we had done with our paddles.

A few minutes later we were out of the whitewater. We had saved time and provided great entertainment for our fellow paddlers who had chosen to portage the rapids. But, the experience had taken years off the life of my canoe and my own cardiovascular system.

Lost on the way to the potty

I was lost.

A tinge of panic swept through my body like the chill you feel getting out of your sleeping bag on a frosty fall morning.

I had lost my way deep in the Canadian wilderness. I had suddenly realized how lousy trees are as landmarks. When your lost they all look the same no matter which direction you turn.

The frightening aspects of my predicament soon gave way to another emotion: embarrassment. I came to the realization that should I be found, the first question my rescuers would ask is whatever possessed me to wander off from a camp in unfamiliar terrain.

My answer would be less than heroic.

"Uh, I had to go to the bathroom."

Mine would not be a story one would find between the covers of *Outdoor Life* or even *People* magazine. However, it might find its way into some trashy newspaper under the headline:

"POTTY BREAK TURNS INTO NIGHTMARE."

(Wildwoods Press) Ontario, Canada-- A 36-year-old Wausau, WI man spent five days in the woods after losing his way to the latrine.

"I just wanted a little privacy," said the embarrassed camper.

He blamed his plight on a slight miscalculation with his compass. Canadian officials were less sympathetic. "If Wisconsin people are as dumb as this guy, they have no business in Canada. The trees are less dense," said one rescuer.

Actually, I'm pretty good with a compass.

A few years back I bought myself one of those orienteering compasses and a book on how to use it. After skimming through the book, I planted myself in the Underdown region of Lincoln County and proceeded to navigate myself through the dense hardwood forest.

I wandered about 50 yards from the road, took a south heading, took about twenty steps, took a west heading, took another 20 steps, took a north heading and two minutes later found myself at the county road where my car was parked.

I felt that was sufficient training and put my compass away until my annual Canadian canoeing-fishing trip.

It was just before suppertime that nature called. I quietly walked off from the campfire, grabbed my TP (outdoorsman jargon for toilet paper) and pulled out the compass from underneath my shirt. I walked about 40 yards from camp, just far enough to be inconspicuous, and then headed north. I chose that direction because directly south of my position was the river.

My eyes affixed to the little red pointer, I tramped my way through the brush for what seemed like a 100 yards. In retrospect it was more like 50 yards. I looked back and could no longer see the camp. Ah, privacy at last I said as I looked for an appropriate commode, which in the woods translates into any fallen log with smooth bark and no bugs.

Upon completing my mission, I picked up the compass hanging from a leather cord around my neck and turned until the little red needle pointed south. I picked up my TP and began walking.

I wasn't two minutes into my trip when I suddenly realized the terrain didn't look at all familiar.

But, compasses never lie, I told myself. The first rule of orienteering is always trust your compass.

Then it hit me.

I had forgotten to turn the directional ring around the needle housing. What I thought was south was actually north, or thereabouts.

I turned 180 degrees and reset my compass to south, the direction I had hoped would lead me to the river. That was assuming that I had correctly set my compass prior to my ill-fated journey. For all I knew, the river could be west of my position.

At least in the city you have street signs. If you're at 44th Street and after a bit of a walk find yourself at 43rd Street, you can reasonably assume that if you walk another 43 blocks in the same direction you'll either run out of city or end up staring at a river.

But, in the woods there is no such organization.

Well, why didn't I just look for the sun? You ask. Even though it was still daylight, the sun was hiding somewhere behind a tall and impenetrable curtain of trees.

I listened intently for the sounds of camp. Unfortunately, the guys I go camping with don't believe in packing boom boxes. About the only sounds they make is dropping an overheated pan on the ground. And, the blasted river flowed as quietly as a feather in the wind.

I'm the kind of man who assesses a situation and immediately begins pondering the nature of my demise. I suspected they would eventually find my body propped up against a maple tree, a roll of toilet paper neatly hanging from one of my boney fingers.

Immersed in this less than optimistic mode of thought, I failed to notice the moose trail I was following had disappeared over the bank of the river. I found myself splashing into salvation.

Ah, but which way to go, upstream or downstream. Fifty-fifty, heck you don't get odds like that in Vegas. I knew I started my woodland walk upstream from camp. That meant camp was probably downstream from my current position. However, given my luck that afternoon, I figured that it would be best to do exactly opposite whatever seemed to be the most logical alternative. I walked upstream.

Two minutes later, camp was in sight.

"What took you so long," one of my compatriots asked.

"You wouldn't believe it. I found this huge patch of blueberries and well, I was going to bring them back for blueberry pancakes, but I got hungry and ate them all."

They believed me.

A look inside a writer's cellblock

Ever wonder what process creates the stories which appear in outdoor magazines. What is it that makes an outdoor writer tick.

Once I described what it's like to write about a beautiful beach somewhere in Wisconsin...

As a public service to my reader, I offer this exclusive glimpse into the mind of an outdoor writer.

Our writer is sitting on a small knoll overlooking a tiny beach on some pristine lake. At the moment he seems to be staring off into space.

Crashing through the cranium, we enter the right lobe of his brain. It looks like an office building with several floors. We enter the structure, walk up to the third floor and down the hall.

We come upon a door on which is painted "WRITING DEPARTMENT." Across the hall, in the office of Lust, a phone rings.

(The lust office is always located across the hall from the writing office, which explains why so many titillating novels are written today).

A fat little cell smoking an ugly cigar jumps on the phone.

"Yeah, whadaya want," he barks.

"Eyes here, we think we've spotted something for you--hang on."

"I'm awaiting your images," the cell says as he turns to a huge screen. On the screen appears a young girl walking along the beach.

"Holy Mackerel!" The cell jumps to his feet and beckons other cells in his office to gather round.

"Will you look at that! She must have had that tan painted on!" All the cells begin bouncing around madly, tipping over chairs, throwing wastepaper cans in the air, yelling and screaming.

Across the hall things are mighty quiet.

Seated on all sides of a long table are cells of all shapes and sizes, each wearing a turtleneck T-shirt and torn blue jeans. Each cell has his title emblazoned across the front of his shirt.

INSPIRATION is pacing the floor.

"I think if we really try we can capture the mood of this lakeside scene--yes, Summer Sun-Beach Fun," INSPIRATION says.

"Sounds plausible--what do we got?" says REASONING.

EXPERIENCE stands up.

"I've got a lot of images, although the eyes seem to be distracted at the moment. I've got these visuals: A shimmering blue lake, its waves clipped with diamonds of light from a noonday sun--tall pine trees swaying in the breeze--a fisherman in a boat--a great blue heron..."

At the head of the table a large, balding cell rises. He's the EDITOR.

"Let's go with it, guys. VOCABULARY, let's get going..."

"Gotcha, chief-- A hot fiery sun beat down on a languid lake scene..."

"That's beats, jerk-- how many times do I have to tell you, the verb has to agree with your subject," GRAMMAR screams.

"That's the sappiest start to a story I've ever heard. That's juvenile stuff, Voc, pure sixth grade," whines INSECURITY.

"How do you expect me to think with all that noise across the hall!" VOCABULARY yells as he glares at INSECURITY.

"Hey, guys, we've got to get this done. Anyway, it seems our brain's interest in writing has been waning ever since EYES locked onto some distraction," the EDITOR says dryly.

VOCABULARY: "A heron's hurried cry drifts through the verdant pines and awakens a languid lakeside scene. A fisherman turns his head from an idle pole..."

EDITOR: "That's great."

"Great? Only great? It's tremendous--readers are going to drool over this. This has got to be the best piece of writing we've ever done," EGO says as he jumps wildly.

"It's so-so--definitely not as good as the stuff put out by that Milwaukee Journal writer," INSECURITY replies.

Meanwhile, across the hall, LUST and all his friends are being hauled out of their office by two big burly cells. It seems someone called CONSCIENCE and FIDELITY to break up the party in Lust's office.

Finding the perfect potty

Many outdoor writers spin stories about catching big fish or shooting trophy bucks.

Others spend page after page describing the beauty of nature and the activities of its woodland creatures.

Still others write book after book on surviving in the wilderness, how to live off tree bark and creek water for weeks on end.

But, I am perhaps the only outdoor writer who would dare to write about outhouses and describe the pleasures of going potty in the pines.

Before you dismiss this particular essay as digusting, I urge you to continue on. I promise I will be discreet.

One thing I hate about public campgrounds are the toilet facilities. I'm sorry, but they smell. They not only smell, they reek.

And, you're never alone in one.

I remember the first outhouse I ever visited. I was about 10 and staying with my best friend in a cottage his parents owned in Northern Wisconsin.

At first I thought it was pretty neat having a little house as a bathroom. Then I sat down on the plywood seat and began having second thoughts. Actually, calling it a seat is an overstatement. It was a plywood board with a hole cut into its center.

Anyway, when I sat down I happened to look up toward the ceiling and to my horror discovered the biggest spider webs I had ever seen. I figured the creatures which constructed them must have had backsides as big as quarters. Although I didn't see any spiders, I was so frightened I all but forgot my reason for being in there.

Then I heard this buzzing sound.

I looked around, but I didn't see any flies or mosquitoes.

I listened more intently.

Suddenly I realized the buzzing was not coming from the air above me, but the darkness below me. I shot up and whipped around just in time to see an angry yellowjacket rise out of the outhouse hole.

I burst through the door and took off running, well, actually hopping. My pants were still wrapped below my knees. After I had made it back to the cabin, I vowed to suffer the pain of constipation rather than return to that little building again.

In the wilderness there are no outhouses, no primitive toilets, no nothing. It's great because suddenly the great outdoors becomes your own private outhouse.

Some campers just traipse off into the woods to do their duty.

Not me.

I select my potty with great care. I have been known to spend a half an hour searching for the right spot.

You see, not just any log will do.

It must be so many inches thick and have smooth bark. I once settled for a log with a less than desirable diameter and suffered a rather messy fall.

I prefer a spot in a small clearing surrounded on three sides by young pines. They not only provide a modicum of privacy, but a certain aroma not found in even the best of bathrooms.

The ground should be covered with moss and have a scattering of small flowers.

But, most important, the spot I choose must have a view.

I tell you, some of the most enjoyable times I have experienced in the Canadian wilderness have been while sitting in my rustic restroom.

I have spent many enjoyable minutes watching the clouds sail by and the birds flit about the tree limbs. I have watched loons on lakes and hawks in flight.

I have been harrassed by squirrels and my privacy invaded by grouse.

My trips have sometimes proved adventurous (as noted in another essay elsewhere in this chapter), but more often have been peaceful and tranquil meditations.

Then again, there was that time I ate one too many wild blueberries.

Hunting with my cat, Lance

One of the prerequisites of becoming an outdoor writer is owning a dog.

A dog that you can write affectionate stories about. Tales in which you can assign near human qualities to otherwise lowly canines. Romantic tales about of walking across a pasture with "King" as a pheasant explodes out of corn field and grouse scurry for cover in thick underbrush.

In fact, the stereotype of an outdoor writer is a man sitting at a typewriter with his faithful canine companion asleep at his feet.

Well, I don't own a dog.

I had a Labrador retriever when I was a kid, but he wasn't anything to write home about when it came to hunting.

A couple years ago I thought about getting another dog, but my wife wanted a cat instead.

Cats are generally useless to outdoor writers.

Most cats abhor the outdoors.

And, with the exception of chasing mice and little birds, cats don't hunt.

I can just imagine trying to write an article for *Outdoor Life* about one's cat...

Hunting the Big Mice

It just after sunrise on a foggy, damp Wisconsin morning. My cat, Lance, and I were tracking the trophy mice which roam in the backyard of my house in Wausau, an area known for producing the rodents you can write home to mother about.

Suddenly Lance's ears perked up, his soft black fur straightened and he purred softly.

"Yeah, I see em, too, ol' boy," I replied as I carefully slid a .22 long into the chamber of my Winchester.

Lance stood perfectly still, his keen senses surveying the thick underbrush ahead of us. "You know, Lance, one of these days I ought to mow this lawn." I whispered. Lance looked up at me with those big yellow feline eyes. "Yes, I know it would ruin the mouse hunting, but the neighbors are starting to complain."

For many minutes we stood perfectly still. Stalking the big mice takes a lot of patience. Mice are wily and spook easily.

It is truly an impressive sight watching a good mouser work a backyard. Cats like Lance are extremely disciplined hunters. And, if they are well-trained, a good mouser can mean the difference between getting your limit or going home with an empty game pouch.

Lance purred again and raised her left paw in the direction of a small arborvitae.

I slowly raised the rifle to my shoulder and made one last adjustment to the 3-9x scope.

Fortunately we were downwind of the big beast and I had plenty of time to take aim. I knew it would be a difficult shot. If I was just a little left of center, there was a very good chance the bullet would kill my rusting lawnmower.

I made one last check of wind direction and fired.

The bullet struck the mouse just above the left shoulder blade, a good clean hit. Those hours of practicing at the range really paid off.

"Fetch, Lance, fetch 'er boy!"

Lance's back arched sharply and his hair stood straight up as he took off through the dew covered grass.

"With whistle commands, I directed Lance through the tall grass to the lifeless mouse. Minutes later the proud little kitty had retrieved a beautiful 14 ounce grey mouse which I put along with the others in the game pouch inside my hunting vest.

It was another triumph in teamwork between a man and his cat."

I have a feeling such a story would not get to first base with the editors of *Outdoor Life* or *Field and Stream*.

He was a lover not a hunter

Many outdoor writers spend endless pages recalling their youth and those carefree days of hunting with their first dog.

I'm sorry, I can't do that.

Yeah, I had a dog once. He was a black Labrador we called Judo. No, he didn't have any unusal martial arts skills. The name was derived by combining the first two letters of my first name with the first two letters of my sister's first name: Ju for Judy, Do for Don. Clever, huh?

We were also advised when we got the dog to limit his name to two syllables. It would make it easier to call out commands during a hunt or field trial, we were told.

My dad and I thought about training Judo to become a field trial champion. I had worked at number of field trials. I was one of the kids who stood in a john boat in the middle of a mosquito infested marsh throwing bound ducks into the weeds. From my point of view, retrieving ducks didn't look all that hard for the dogs provided they paid attention to their master's whistles.

But, as hard as my father and I tried, we could never get Judo to obey voice or whistle commands. And, training him to heel was a real adventure.

I was all of 90 pounds at the time and Judo was somewhere in the 50 to 75 pound range. Every time I tried to train him to heel, he'd end up dragging me down the sidewalk.

Once we took him out into a field to see if he'd actually retrieve something. We threw a ball about 20 yards out and he went right for it. My dad and I turned to one another with renewed hope we might have a useful dog. But, instead of retrieving the ball, the black lab just keep going and going.

He returned to the car about 30 minutes later.

One time we took him pheasant hunting and he retrieved a skunk. I tell you, you haven't lived until you have driven in a car with dog covered with skunk odor sitting in the backseat. Rolling down all the windows does little to lessen the unbearable smell.

Took him duck hunting once. He spent the whole time jumping out of the boat and swimming around the lilly pads. When one of us finally did shoot a duck, the mutt refused to leave the boat to fetch it. Although, toward the end of the day, Judo did successfully retrieve a decoy.

One thing Judo was good at was tracking down woodchucks and chipmunks.

Judo was great with chipmunks. It wasn't that he actually hunted them; it was more like he played with them. Judo was more a lover than a hunter.

As soon as you let him out of the pen, he'd race to the woodpile and begin taking it apart log by log until he found the chipmunk hiding inside.

A few minutes later a chipmunk would shoot out of the woodpile, race across the lawn with Judo in close pursuit and seek refuge in the nearest downspout.

Undeterred, Judo would commence to rip apart the aluminum pipe.

First, he'd clamp down the end. Then he'd jump on the pipe to knock it off the side of the house. After accomplishing that, he'd clamp down the other end and play with the section of pipe like a big stick. Meanwhile, the chipmunk would be racing back and forth in the pipe, its little claws scrapping on the metal like fingernails on a blackboard.

Every so often my dad would get these angry calls from neighbors.

"Oakland, get over here right now! Your blasted black dog is tearing into my downspouts again. He's already destroyed three and is in the process of ripping apart a fourth. And, I've got all these dead chipmunks in my backyard. Either you get your behind over here or I'm calling the cops and the dog catcher!"

I swear every house in the neighborhood got new downspouts because of Judo.

But, that isn't a story worthy of *Field and Stream*.

The sinister skipper

"Let's go sailing. There's an ad in here for an outfit that rents sailboat rides," my wife said as she put down a vacation brochure.

"How much?"

"Only $20 per person for a three-hour sail," she said with increasing enthusiasm.

"I don't know, it seems awfully expensive," I said.

"Come on, be adventurous for once in your life," she snapped back.

"Isn't there something a little less expensive, maybe a raft ride or something."

"Look, I'll buy the tickets."

"Well, if you insist. I guess it is ship ahoy," I said turning back to my newspaper.

A week later we found ourselves on this rickety little pier looking down at this disgustingly small sailboat.

"Gee dear," I said nervously. " I thought this was suppose to be, well, you know, a yatch."

Just then a small, bearded man popped out from the sailboat's miniscule cabin. He struck me as looking somewhat like Norman Bates.

"Welcome to Captain Jack's sailboat rides and pierside pizza palace. Want a pier baked pizza, mister?"

"Uh, we've just come about the sailboat rides," I replied.

"Great, glad to have you aboard. But, can I interest you in a pizza. Order it now and I'll have it ready when you return. Most people prefer it that way. I mean, it's a bear getting seasick with peperoni in your belly," he said as he glanced overboard.

"No, we just want the ride," I replied.

"Suit yourself, but it's not everyday you can get a pizza on a pier," he said.

A mother and her two teenage daughters showed up at the pier. With their arrival, the skipper put on a white cap and proudly announced the excursion was about to begin. He glanced up at billowing cumulus clouds parading across the horizon.

"Yup mates, it's going to be one helluva of a ride when my sails taste the winds in those babies," he said with a sinster laugh.

I was about to tell the skipper I wanted to call it quits when I realized the boat was already 100 yards offshore. The thin little man tugged at a couple of ropes and suddenly the sails exploded open. The hull of the boat instantly tilted what seemed like 90 degrees.

"Ah, don't worry mates, she'll never tip. She's got 1,000 pounds of lead in her belly," the skipper said as he wrestled with the rudder.

Great, if this thing goes over I'll be buried under a ton of lead, I said to myself as I hung on for dear life.

The boat sliced through the water at increasingly faster speeds.

"LOOK OUT YOU JERK," the skipper cried out as the sailboat nearly cut in half a windsurfer. "Bunch of hotrodding punks is all they are," he grumbled.

At one time I had thoughts of taking pictures of our leisurely cruise. Instead I found myself hugging the boat deck and praying that a sudden shift in the wind wouldn't send me sailing overboard.

"Isn't this great," the skipper exclaimed. "Sailing really works up an appetite. Sure you wouldn't want that pizza?"

About all I wanted at that point was a Dramamine and a shot of whiskey.

Why I don't hunt deer

"You hunt?"

It is a question I'm usually asked come mid November. Usually I respond with a retelling of this story of one boy's fateful trip into the woods.

When I was in high school, I looked forward to fall when I could drive up to public hunting grounds near Mazomanie and hunt squirrel along the banks of the Wisconsin River.

I liked squirrel hunting because you could do it sitting down. I'd find myself a comfortable stump to lean against, prop up my gun and fall fast asleep.

When I'd awaken from my nap, invariably there would be a squirrel rustling about the leaves above me.

Given my somewhat groggy state, I usually missed him no matter how many bullets I sent his way.

One year I decided to take up bow hunting. I got myself a 50 pound recurve bow and a half dozen razorhead arrows and headed off into the woods.

I had shot bow and arrow before; however, I wasn't prepared for a bow with a 50 pound pull. Being a rather scrawny kid, it took everything I had to draw back that arrow.

I was kind of nervous that day because I was hunting alone and I wasn't quite sure what I would do with a deer if I should happen to shoot one.

Oh, I had read a dozen books on bow hunting, but I realized there is a heck of a lot of difference between reading about gutting a deer and actually doing it. I mean, you don't learn brain surgery from reading a book.

Anyway, I was walking through a stand of oak when suddenly my eyes caught a patch of brown to my left. I slowly turned and there, a mere 25 yards away, was this awesome buck.

I about dropped my bow.

Slowly, ever so slowly, I raised my bow and drew back the arrow. My arms shook from muscle strain and nervousness as I held that string back for what seemed like an eternity. I aimed and re-aimed and aimed again.

I knew I would only have one shot at glory and, darn it, I wasn't going to choke.

I took a deep breath and let go of the string.

The arrow shot through some brush, flew right over the back of the buck and landed dead center in the trunk of a young oak tree.

My first chance at a deer and I shoot a $%$#%!! tree.

It was the last time I would see a deer that day and that season. And, it was the last time I ever went bow hunting. Shooting a tree will do that to you.

In college I tried a little gun hunting, but that ended when I encountered a slight problem with my first buck.

"Hey! What stinks," my roommate said as he walked into our dorm room. Suddenly he stopped dead.

"Oh lordy! What's that deer doing hanging above my bed!" he screamed.

"Will you shut up, you'll have the resident assistants down on us," I shot back.

"Oakland, you've got to get that thing outta here. Geez look at all the flies."

"Hey, if I take it outside, somebody will steal it for sure. Here make yourself useful," I said as I handed my roommate a flyswatter.

"How'd you get this thing in here?"

"Hey, if I can smuggle two cases of Old Style into the room on a Saturday night, a deer is a piece of cake," I said proudly.

About 3 a.m. that night my roommate and I pushed the carcass out of our second floor window and into my roommate's pickup truck.

The next morning the dorm was crawling with police and university officials. I asked a cop I knew what was up.

"Seems some lady driving by last night reported seeing someone being pushed out of a dorm window. She said two men in a pickup truck drove off with the body. Know anything about it?"

I shook my head meekly and walked away.

It was at that moment I gave up deer hunting for good.

TP Don't leave home without it

As an experienced woodsman, I feel obligated to offer a bit of outdoor advice, something to help those who only occasionally venture from civilization.

Outdoor books tell you to buy the best boots, the warmest sleeping bag and the most waterproof tent around. They tell you what food to take. Some offer survival skills.

But, they all forget to tell you one important thing: Don't leave the world of indoor plumbing without a good supply of toilet paper.

Your health depends on it.

I'm not kidding.

One year, when my pack was unusually full, I decided I'd cut back on the amount of TP I planned to take into the wilderness. Who needs a whole roll for a week in the woods, I told myself. So I spent the next 30 minutes unraveling a roll of Charmin until it was about half the width.

Two days into the trip I developed what could politely be called intestinal distress. I rolled off toilet paper as fast as paper through a high speed computer printer.

Three days into the trip I was TP-less.

It's amazing how friends will take advantage of you in such a situation.

"Hey, can I borrow a little TP," I asked my brother-in-law.

"How much?"

"How about the roll?"

"You've got to be kidding," he said as he turned his attention to the campfire.

"Okay, a half of roll."

He continued to stare into the fire.

"A foot?"

He shook his head.

"Three sheets."

"Two."

"Deal!" I yelled as I clutched my gut and watched my knees buckle.

Having learned my lesson, the following year I took an entire roll of the softest toilet paper I could find. I felt very secure in the woods that trip. That is until it rained.

I never knew toilet paper could soak up so much water. It lay in my backpack like some engorged sponge.

"Oakland, for crying out loud, you can't do that," my father-in-law said shaking his head.

"I'm a desperate man," I replied.

"Do you realize what would happen if someone came by, particularly someone with warden in front of his name."

"Look, either I dry out this TP or its leaf city the rest of the trip. Remember last year I tried that. My wife still laughs when she recalls that poison ivy rash on my behind. My doctor couldn't stop laughing long enough to treat it. I couldn't sit down and worse, I couldn't itch it."

"But, stringing toilet paper from tree limbs isn't the answer," he told me. "Try drying the sheets out over the fire. If it works for socks, it will work for toilet paper."

So that night I sat by the fire and held a length of toilet paper between sticks I held in both hands. Every so often, I'd get to close and the TP would explode into flame.

"Ass to ashes, dust to dust," my brother-in-law laughed.

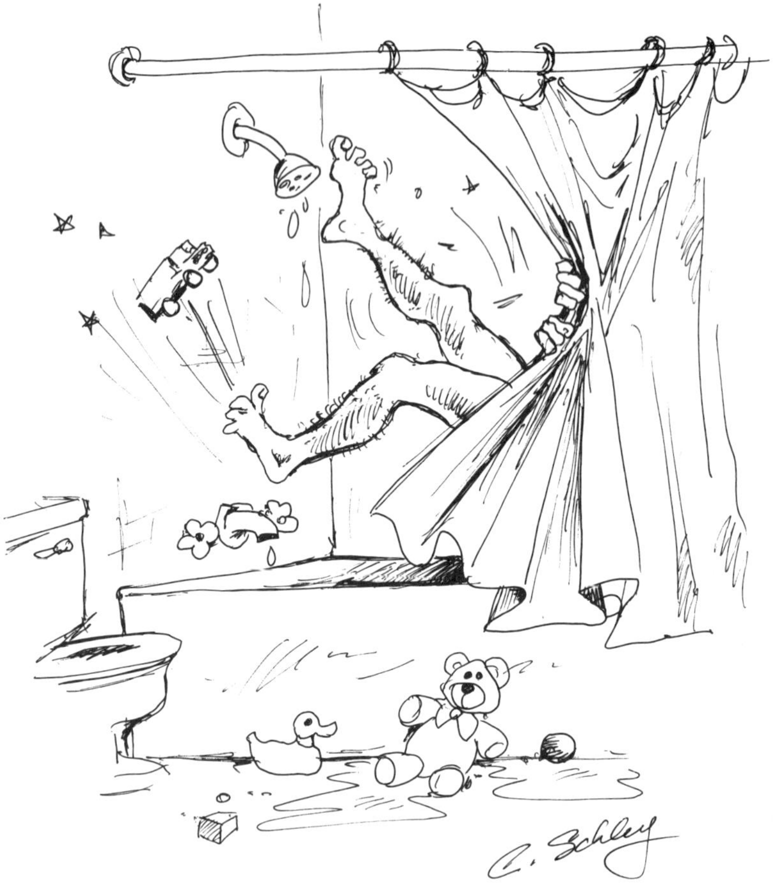
C. Schley

Chapter Two

Toys make tub treacherous

There once was a time in the years B.C. (Before Children) when a shower was something less than an adventure.

Now before I take a shower, my wife inquires if my life insurance is paid up.

When I was living alone, the shower was a place where one cleaned the body and, at least in the morning, awakened the spirit. It was a relaxing prelude to an otherwise hectic day. It was a chance to exercise one's latent vocal abilities without fear of snide criticism (except when one lived in a thin walled apartment building).

Today, the shower is an obstacle course worthy of Marine boot camp.

The trouble is my two daughters believe the bathtub is their own personal playground. Getting clean is secondary to having a good time. Soap is something to be avoided at all costs (except expensive bubble bath which they can't get enough of).

Now, I'm not talking about playing with a rubber ducky. Next to the tub is a plastic crate filled with toys. When my daughters take a bath, the eldest picks up the crate and empties the contents into their little white tub. It's amazing the two kids can find room to soak.

The consequence of all this can be best related in the retelling of one horrible morning I suffered a couple of weeks ago.

It was shortly after 6 a.m. As usual I was running late. I dashed into the kitchen, literally threw two eggs into a pot full of water, whipped the range dial to high, and sprinted back to the bathroom hoping to complete my shower before the boiled eggs exploded.

Half awake I jumped into what I thought would be a dry tub.

IIIIEEEEEEEEEAAAAAH!

Instead of dry fiberglass, my feet hit about two inches of water chilled by the night air. I looked down and discovered a washcloth covering the drain, the same washcloth I used the night before to scrub the kids.

I opened the faucet and stood shivering until the water got hot, too hot. It was a terrible dilemma. Do I scald my body to warm my feet or do I risk hypothermia by leaving my feet immersed in ice cold water?

Well, at least I was wide awake.

Soon the water reached a comfortable temperature and I was able to resume my morning bathing ritual.

To understand what happened next, you have to know that I'm terribly nearsighted. Without my glasses I have a tendency to walk into things. Generally, this poses no problem in the shower because there isn't much one can run into in a bathtub.

Unless you have children.

"AAAAAAARGH!"

I actually can't remember which was louder, my scream or the crash my body made as it ricochetted off the glass shower door and careened into the base of the tub.

It didn't really matter. Both prematurely awakened my 16-month-old and my 3-year-old and the two of them abruptly ended my wife's sleep.

"Donald! What happened?" my wife said as she rushed into the bathroom.

"I don't know," I said as I grabbed a towel and wrapped it around my crumpled body. "When I took a step toward the soap dish, my foot landed on something hard and sharp, almost like a rock you inadvertently step on while wading across an unfamiliar beach. Give me my glasses!"

My wife handed me my somewhat fogged glasses and I discovered that I had been standing in what appeared to be a giant toy box. The floor of the tub was covered with plastic blocks, toy boats, marbles, soggy dolls and an assortment of toy trucks and cars.

"Daddy, you broke my truck!" my 3-year-old screamed as she scooted past her mother.

I lifted my body off the plastic truck. The weight of my back had flattened it into three or four pieces. One of the wheels was wedged between two of my toes.

I shut off the water and limped out of the tub.

"What's that noise?" my wife asked.

It sounded like an overheated radiator.

"My eggs!"

I ran to the kitchen and watched as tiny bits of cooked egg were carried out of the pot, across the stove and onto the floor by a lava like flow of boiling water, water which found its way to my bare feet.

By the time my wife had applied first aid ointment to my reddened toes, I had missed not only breakfast but my bus, too.

I couldn't bring myself to call my boss and tell him I'd be a little late that morning. My wife did the honors.

"Yes, Donald will be in late. He had some trouble in the shower this morning...what trouble, well, I rather not say...I'm sure he'll tell you about it when he gets there..."

At that moment, I wished I had called in sick.

Father's Day is for real saints

Instead of a pat on the back, I should have received a medal for Father's Day. There were moments when I doubted whether I would survive it.

The day got off to a fast and early start when my then 2-year-old daughter came racing into our bedroom shortly after 7 a.m. Had I not been out until after midnight the night before, I would have appreciated her wake up call a little more than I actually did.

"Daddy, wake up! DADDY, WAKE UP," she screamed as she pulled on my hair.

"Daddy's dead, go away," I mumbled half asleep.

Nevertheless she persisted. I guess a 2-year-old figures if she is awake, then everybody else in the house should also be up. That's undoubtedly why, after waking us up, the little terror charged into the baby's room.

I shot out of bed in the hopes of catching her before she awakened the sleeping screamer. And I would have, had I not tripped over those building blocks my eldest daughter had left in the hallway the night before. Thank goodness I landed in that basket of dirty laundry.

I could tell that my special day was going to indeed be special when my 2-year-old daughter decided to play waitress and bring me my morning coffee. Unfortunately, she neglected to factor into her otherwise noble gesture the weight of the coffee mug. She delivered the brew to my bare feet via the floor express.

Sensing my emotional state was of questionable stability, my wife suggested we all go to the beach for a Father's Day picnic and swim.

"What a super idea," I told her. Heck, what better present for dear ol' dad than an afternoon at the beach watching all those good-looking girls in their great-looking swimsuits. I didn't tell my wife that. I told her the swim would do me good, even though I had absolutely no intention of going into the water.

Well, my daughters must have sensed my motives were less than pure, for they combined their toddler talents to deny me this one pleasure left to a dad my age.

Instead of girlwatching, I spent the whole afternoon playing lifeguard to the 2-year-old while trying to keep the the little one from screaming. If that wasn't bad enough, the 2-year-old figured every toy on the beach was hers and was constantly carting off other kids' plastic buckets and shovels.

When she tried to make off with one of those big rubber boats, I said enough was enough and informed my wife that either we were leaving, or our daughter was going to get busted.

At that point, I figured the worst of the day was over.

Then my 2-year-old shoved a button up her nose.

Don't ask me where she got the button. All I know is she came up to me and pointed to something inside one nostril. I didn't panic. I did what any rational father would do.

"Dear! Your daughter has a button up her nose, do something!"

Upon returning from the hospital emergency room, my wife informed me that our daughter had provided the ER staff with some much appreciated comic relief. She said the doctor could hardly control his chuckling when he asked my daughter, "Got anymore up there?"

Yes sir, I should have gotten a medal that day.

Daughter's debut has dad in a dither

I'm a lousy backstage father.

My youngest daughter was four months old when she played baby Jesus in the Christmas pageant at the First Presbyterian Church in Wausau.

Her selection was more out of convenience than good looks or acting ability. She just happened to be a baby who was available and not under contract to any other church.

We didn't plan it that way.

I mean, nine months before, I didn't snuggle up to my wife and suggest that if we tried for a second child that night, the baby would have a good chance at starring in the Christmas pageant.

I had no objection to my daughter's shot at stardom. Heck, if I don't have to change diapers, I'll go along with just about anything.

My role in all this was to hold the baby backstage and then hand her to "Mary" at the appropriate point in the play.

A seemingly simple assignment, yet there was a lot of strategy involved.

For example, just before leaving for the church we fed the baby. Not a full meal, but just enough to sort of mellow her out. We didn't want to put her to sleep, because she might awaken at a most inopportune moment in the play.

Despite our planning, things did not start out well.

The minute we put the baby into the car, she screamed and never stopped screaming the whole way to the church.

I started to get an empty, pre-ulcerous feeling in my stomach.

When we arrived at the church, she miraculously settled down. But, when the pastor came in and announced the play was to begin, the baby started crying again.

I tried holding her in a dozen different ways. I uttered utterly ridiculous things into her ears. I swayed like a willow branch as I rocked her in my arms. Nothing worked.

I bent one finger and stuck the knuckle in her mouth. She began sucking it. When she realized that a knuckle doesn't produce milk, she started screaming again.

I had to play my ace.

I grabbed the bottle from my pocket and shoved it into her mouth. It worked. All was quiet.

Suddenly "Mary" came through the stage door. I handed her the baby and the two disappeared through the door.

My nerves tightened like a tug-of-war rope as I waited for that first terribly embarrassing cry, that ear-piercing sound that would obliterate all else-- dialog, song, everything.

I wasn't worried for myself. I could handle it. If she started crying, I'd just disappear into the nearest men's room, lock myself in a stall and put toilet paper in my ears.

No, I was worried for her. I mean, people don't forget the child who ruined the Christmas pageant. All through life, my daughter would have people coming up to her saying, "Why, I remember when you were a little baby, especially the time you absolutely destroyed the Presbyterian Church's Christmas play by crying louder than most choir members could sing. Heh, heh."

I was suffering. You see, when I get nervous, I don't pace or start talking to myself. No, I just stand there quietly and turn my insides to mush.

My stomach suffers the most. Any food within it is instantly vaporized into gas... gas which somehow must be released from the body.

There I stood with this horrible feeling that just as the congregation would reach a quiet moment in the play, that building pressure would be relieved with an awesome discharge. All eyes would turn from the pageant to the door at stage right. "Good lord, what was that?" they'd mumble to each other.

To make matters worse, the pageant seemed to progress in slow motion. "Come on people, sing faster, don't you realize you have a ticking time bomb on stage," I said under my breath.

Finally "Mary" came through the door with an awake but quiet baby in her arms.

It was a miracle, I tell you.

I wholly expected streams of light from the ceiling, a celestial choir singing and a booming voice saying "You owe me, Donald Oakland."

Clang of pots, pans, not music to sup by

Dr. Spock where are you when I need you the most?

You taught me about teething.

You detailed diaper rash.

So, how come you never taught me how to feed a toddler supper.

Supper at the Oakland household is always a lively affair. We have a kid who would make John Belushi's food fighting in Animal House look like a Miss Manner's society tea.

Around food, my 3-year-old is awesome.

You haven't lived until you've witnessed a half of a peach fly across the entire length of a kitchen, splat against the side of a cupboard drawer and then slowly slide down into a bowl of mashed potatoes.

My wife usually takes charge of supper. I play the gofer."Donald! Pick that bowl up off the floor... Donald! Get me a washcloth before the spaghetti in the kid's hair dries."

I'm completely lost when the wife decides to spend the evening away from home.

A dog I can handle if tablescraps are plentiful. If there is a can of cat food around, I can cope with a kitty. But, neither is appropriate for the feeding of a small child.

My wife always leaves me with a list of things to feed our two young daughters. I usually ignore the list because A) I'm too tired to cook anything and B) I'd never find the ingredients anyway.

So, I wrestle the kids into their chairs and head for the refrigerator for whatever qualifies as edible that day.

I give the kids the "A" stuff, that is food which I'm reasonably certain was leftover from the night before. That leaves me with the "B" stuff, the food of unknown origin and of questionable toxicity.

When my wife feeds the kids, she lays out each serving on their plates and allows the children to feed themselves.

Although I admire such independence, I don't encourage it when facing a 1 year-old one on one.

See, I know what the kid will do. About halfway through her meal she'll decide mealtime is over and playtime has begun. With one swoop of her forearm, she'll have that entire tray of food on the floor. Meanwhile, the 3-year-old has spilled an entire glass of milk.

I choose an alternative method of feeding the little one. I take as much food as I figure it will take to fill her up, throw it all in the Cuisinart and puree it to a pulp.

Then I take a spoon and shovel the mash into her mouth like a fireman throwing coal into the boiler of a steam locomotive. Before the kid knows what hit her, supper is over with.

Then it is my turn to eat.

Suppertime is when children get even with their parents for all the nasty things mom and dad did to them during the day.

Like I'm just about to finish my twice leftover hamburger, when the kids suddenly start opening drawers and pulling out every kitchen utensil.

I remind them that such youthful enterprise is not appreciated and then turn my attention to an aged potato.

Suddenly the room explodes as a full set of metal bowls bounce off the floor. The crashing sound tenses me up like a coiled rattler and causes a piece of potato to lodge itself in my throat.

The kids in one spectacular display of kitchenware pyrotechnics have doomed me to a night of indigestion.

I try to appease the little ones with a dessert of lime Jell-O. So what do they do. One takes a mouthful of the stuff, asks for a glass of milk and then spits the whole works back into the glass. The sight of that green goop floating like an Irish iceberg in the milk nearly sends me to the bathroom.

Meanwhile, the older girl flicks a glop of Jell-O dead-center into the kitchen window.

Just as I finish off my second glass of Alka-Selzer, the 1-year-old comes scooting into the room with a look and smell that tells me a rather ugly diaper needs changing.

I can think of no horror worse than changing a diaper on a full stomach.

I tell you, fatherhood is not for the squeamish.

Dear? Why is there salt in our bed?

There are times when I wonder if I'll survive parenthood. Like when my eldest daughter was 2...

My kid is a born daddy abuser.

It is my sincere belief that the kid has been genetically programmed by some higher authority to make my life less than pleasant.

It is as if I once did something to offend someone, but was never caught doing it. Is my being a parent actually penance for some long forgotten indiscretion?

It's not the kid's fault. I mean, the things she does to me are not learned behavior.

And, 98 percent of the time she is a real loving, adorable child. But, just when you think she is a joy to have around, some invisible hand flicks a switch inside her initiating a programmed response to do some terrible number on dear old dad.

Never to mommy mind you. Everything is directed at dad.

Case in point.

After a hard day at work, I come home expecting to be able to sit down, put my feet up and read a newspaper in peace.

I'm just about to ease into a relaxing read when she charges across the room and literally tackles the newspaper I'm holding.

Instead of a newspaper in my lap, I have a squirming kid on top of crumbled newsprint.

But, that is only the beginning.

While I'm half napping in my easy chair, this little rugrat sneaks up and steals the pens from my pocket.

The kid either has an innate desire to write or is practicing to be the world's greatest pickpocket.

You might think taking daddy's pens is kind of cute. However, the next day when daddy can't find his pens, the cuteness is no longer there.

"Have you seen my pens!" I holler at my sleeping wife as I empty the contents of every drawer in the kitchen.

"Look in the living room," a slightly groggy wife replies.

"I already did," I tell her as I survey the overturned chairs, pillaged bookcase and stripped sofa.

"It must be in the baby's room," I tell myself in an increasingly exasperated voice.

45

"Don't you dare go into the baby's room," my now fully awake wife protests.

"But, she is holding my pens hostage in there!"

Suddenly the kid wakes up screaming. I can hear my wife growling fiercely in the other room.

"Well, I'd better get going or I'll be late for work," I say meekly as I make for the back door.

When I return home that night my wife reads me the riot act for: A) prematurely awakening her and the baby; B) making a shambles of the house, and C) any other of my shortcomings she cares to complain about.

And, through it all, the kid just sits there quietly smiling.

The kid is insidious.

Like the times she takes daddy's beer, runs to the bathroom and proceeds to pour it into the toilet.

One night, after a particularly grueling day, I had just collasped into bed when I felt something gritty. I leaped out of bed and looked down at the mattress.

"Honey, what is salt doing in our bed?"

She didn't answer. My wife was too busy trying to hold back laughing at the sight of me frantically brushing salt from my pajamas and beard.

My body felt like it had been wrapped in fiberglass batting.

After my wife managed to gain some self control, she explained that the kid had swiped the salt shaker from the kitchen and had disappeared. She later found the salt shaker underneath the bed, but didn't think anything of it at the time.

Needless to say, I didn't get much sleep that night. I mean, a mattress that feels like the Sahara Desert is not the most comfortable thing in the world.

I'm going to continue documenting these cases of daddy abuse. And, when I'm a granddaddy and my kids have kids, I'm going to teach their kids a few things to make my grownup kids squirm.

Granny earns a Purple Heart

When I offered to take the kids to grandmother's house, little did I know it would lead to my mother going to the hospital.

I felt pretty proud of myself when I offered to give my wife a weekend of freedom from the kids. And, she was so appreciative she set aside any doubts she had about me surviving a trip to Madison with our children, who at the time were 2 and 6 months old.

The first challenge of this glorious adventure was to get the kids to Madison without all the screaming which usually accompanies such trips.

I had a plan. The morning of the trip, I told my wife not to give either child an afternoon nap. That way, I reasoned, the kids would sleep for most, if not all, of the two and a half hour trip.

And, it worked beautifully.

Two miles out of town and both were asleep in their car seats. Piece of cake, I said with unabashed confidence.

About an hour into the trip something happened that I hadn't anticipated. Car seats are great for safety, but lousy for sleeping. My 2-year-old just couldn't get comfortable and awakened ornery as all heck.

Contingency plan No. 1 immediately went into effect. I whipped out a bag of cheese-flavored popcorn. I figured by giving her one kernel at a time, we'd be in Madison before she stopped snacking.

And, it worked beautifully.... for about a mile.

"My bag!" my daughter cried out.

"No dear, it's daddy's bag. If I give it to you, you'll just ..."

Suddenly the kid grabbed the bag out of my hand and as I fought to regain control of the car, the kid ripped the bag open and threw the popcorn into the air. Next thing I knew I was inside a cloud of popcorn.

"Why did you do THAT!" I yelled. Dumb question. Kids that age don't need reasons for doing things. The only thing my outburst accomplished was waking up my 6-month-old in the backseat.

For the rest of the trip, it was screaming in stereo.

At grandma's house things settled down into a fairly manageable routine. As long as I confined my activities to changing diapers, making bottles and keeping my two daughters occupied, things were relatively peaceful.

That is until my 2-year-old sent grandma to the hospital emergency room.

The 6-month-old was napping upstairs and the 2-year-old was playing with toys downstairs. It seemed like a good time for ol' dad to sneak out of the house and do some big city shopping for an hour or so.

When I returned I found my mother with several big Band-Aids above one eye. It seems that just after I had left, my older daughter got it in her head to wake up my younger daughter. She announced her intentions and took off running for the stairs.

Mother dropped what she was doing and took off after the tyke. She caught her about three steps up the stairs. Unfortunately, in grabbing the child, my mother lost her balance and slammed her head into the wall.

For the rest of the weekend my mother wore a bandage around her head. She looked like she had just returned from a war.

I felt like I should have given her a medal for going one on one with a 2-year-old and living to tell about it.

Holiday fun brings on all-night run

Kids have a way of making parents pay for the fun they have.

On the Fourth of July our family went up north to a friend's cabin to partake in some patriotic partying.

Despite a little rainstorm, we had a good time. The kid had a good time, too.

She partied full tilt all day.

When she wasn't playing in the lake, she was conning someone out of a cookie or sip of pop.

Boy, can my kid manipulate adults.

All it takes is a cute little smile, and like, it's any adult within 10 feet is suddenly at her command. She doesn't have to say a word, just point and it's hers.

She even tried to weasel a sip of beer out of someone.

"Chip off the ol' block," the guy said as he turned toward me, smiled and offered the tyke a pop instead.

Even the bugs didn't slow her down.

We adults were swatting and scratching all day. At one point some of us looked like an African tribe doing some ritual dance on the front lawn.

The day finally drew to a close and we were on our way back home. My wife and I were exhausted.

"Well, at least we won't have any trouble putting her to sleep tonight," I said to my wife as we pulled out of the driveway. The kid was already sound asleep in her car seat.

She slept the entire two and a half hours it took us to get home. I envied her as I battled to stay awake at the wheel.

We got home and were unpacking the car when all of a sudden the little one woke up with a scream, which I translated to mean: "Let's party!"

"No dear, it's time for bed," I said quietly.

"No bed, party-time," she wailed in her own screeching vernacular.

"Daddy's tired, mommy's tired, baby is..."

"Baby just had a two-hour nap and is ready to party hardy again," she cried.

I put the wide-eyed kid to bed and hoped she got the idea that this Fourth of July was history.

No way! Instead of falling asleep, she bellered, screamed and kicked the side of her crib with her feet."

"Go take care of your daughter," I groaned to my wife as I put the covers over my head.

My wife reluctantly got up, picked up the little tyke and went into the living room to rock her into slumberland.

A half an hour later, I heard my wife return. All was quiet.

Ten minutes later the baby's room sounded like Animal House.

"Dear..."

"No way, it's your turn," my wife grumbled.

"But, it's 2:30 in the morning and I've got to go to work tomorrow. I mean, you and the kid can sleep till noon, I've got to get up at 6," I pleaded.

My wife just rolled over and buried her head in the pillow.

I got up and found the kid boogying in bed with her stuffed bear.

"Come on little one, give it a rest," I whined.

She screamed back and threw the teddy bear at me.

The next thing I knew I was in the rocker with her. She wanted to read one of her picture books. I was fighting to stay awake.

A half an hour passed. The kid is tearing around the living room. I'm rocking half unconscious in the chair, scratching the mosquito bites on my legs and listening to the birds awakening outside.

I figure the kid just doesn't want to sleep alone, so I take her into our bedroom. Wrong move, daddy-o. It only succeeded in waking my wife. It was not a pretty sight.

"Your turn," I told my wife as I collapsed onto the mattress.

It was a heavy price a father had to pay that night for taking his family for some holiday fun.

Manhood takes a backseat to silence

I am happy to report I have solved the problem of infant car seats.

Well, sort of solved it.

Heck, next to diaper rash, car seats are the worse thing the under 3 set has to endure.

Well, I discovered the real problem with our kid wasn't that she was strapped into a car seat; it was she disliked being in the back seat.

Put her in the front seat and nary a squawk.

However, her silence didn't come without a price, I discovered.

Putting the kid in the front seat meant that my wife had to move to the back seat.

That didn't sit well with her.

"I can't sit in the back seat, it makes me car sick," she protested as we were about to depart on a trip to Madison.

"But, dear it's either that or listening to a screaming kid for three hours," I said.

"There is another option."

"You're not suggesting I sit in the back seat," I replied hesitantly.

"And, why not?"

"We're talking about my manhood," I said.
"Men don't belong in back seats. Men belong driving.
"Look around you. When you see a man and a woman in a car, how many times is the woman driving? Never."
My wife didn't say a word, but her face began turning noticeably redder.
"Ever since Ford put the first car on the road, men have driven women around, especially when they are husband and wife.
"It is a tradition seemingly immune to the wrath of raging feminists," I continued.
Despite what I thought was flawless logic, I was soon banished to the back seat.
It wasn't pretty.
I soon found myself curled up between a couple of suitcases. My head rested on a plastic garbage bag filled with dirty diapers.
For the next half hour my stomach grumbled. The internal distress was caused partly because of my posture and partly because of the strong odor of soiled diapers. I tell you, diaper odor can penetrate the strongest of plastic bags.
"Dear, do you think you could open the window, I really could use some fresh air," I said between gasps.
"But, if I open the window the baby might catch cold," she replied unsympathetically.
"AAAAAAAARRRRGGH!"
"What's wrong?"
"Oh, nothing dear, just my left leg cramping," I groaned as I lifted a suitcase off my legs.
"Will you be quiet, the baby is sleeping," she scolded.
"Give me air, woman! I feel like I'm living inside a diaper pail," I pleaded.
"That reminds me, since you're not driving, can you change her when she wakes up? The bag of diapers should be back there somewhere."
"Yeah, they're back here all right," I mumbled as I picked them out from under the small of my back.

"And, can you give her some juice?"
"Uh, I don't think so," I replied.
"Why not?"
"Well, I sort of laid on her bottle and the top sort of popped off... and, like I've got apple juice from the back of my neck right down to my..."
"How about her crackers?"
"Crushed." I said as I stared at the cracker bits which the apple juice had cemented to my pants.
It didn't matter. When the baby awakened she was quite content to sit there looking out the window at the passing world. Never once did she turn around to see how her daddy was doing.
Nobody cared daddy was in the back battling to save his male ego and his stomach from a rather ignominous end.

I live in fear of fairs

I live in fear of the day I have to take my daughter to the county fair.
Oh, I don't worry about taking her to the livestock barns. I'd love to show her the rabbits and sheep.
I'd even take her on any ride that my stomach could bear.
But, I dread the day she discovers the midway...
"Daddy, Daddy, I want a teddy bear," she squeals.
"Huh," I say as I pick cotton candy from my beard.
"A big teddy bear like that one," she says pointing to some young fellah who just won his girlfriend a five-foot tall, brilliant lime green bear.
"Uh, I don't think so."
"Why not?"
"They're not for sale."

"Well, sure they are. Look, there are a whole lot of them hanging in that booth over there," she says pointing at one of the midway games.

"Come along dear, I'll buy you a chili dog."

'I WANT A TEDDY BEAR!" she whines as she pulls me toward the game booth.

"Yes, sir, win the little girl a bear," the carney says loudly.

He knows he has me trapped and moves in for the kill.

"All your daddy has to do is put these two balls into that basket and this big red cuddly teddy bear is all yours, little darling," he says in a child-like voice to my wide-eyed daughter.

No, it's not that I don't want to spend a $1 or two trying to win my daughter's everlasting love. It's like I know I'll never succeed. I just can't win at carnival games.

Take for instance what happened to me at a Wisconsin Valley Fair a couple of years ago.

"My wife was getting all nostalgic seeing these young gals carrying soft and fuzzy prizes that their boyfriends had won for them.

"Come on, Donald, win me something," she said with girlish enthusiasm.

"Okay," I said with less than boyish enthusiasm.

Skee-ball looked like something I could win and unlike the other games it was only 50 cents a try. My confidence was bolstered as I watched some young turk rack up hundreds of points with seemingly little effort.

I put my four bits into the slot.

I rolled one ball...10 points. I needed at least 150 to win. I rolled ball two... 10 points... I rolled a third ball....20 points... and a fourth ball. Somehow it landed in the 100 point hole. A WINNER.

For that I got three tickets.

I put in another 50 cents.

I threw six balls and accumulated 120 points.

I put in another 50 cents.

Racked up 80 points.
People were beginning to laugh.
I put in another 50 cents.
My wife tried it. Nice effort but no cigar.

The upshot is I spent $2, got three prize tickets which won me a pair of green shoelaces. I was not only humbled, I was humiliated.

I pressed on.

I tried knocking over three bottles with a ball.

Missed the bottles completely...twice.

Now I was $4 poorer and still had only a pair of green shoelaces to show for it.

I tried to pick up a bottle with a string. That effort lasted less than 10 seconds and cost me another $1.

Something told me I shouldn't try the rifle shoot. In the frame of mind I was in, I might end up shooting myself instead of those impossible stars.

I mean, how would you feel blowing the better part of $10 so that you could give your wife a pair of green shoelaces.

You know what really worries me? The thought of being there with my daughter and suddenly a teenage boy walking up and, with one toss, winning for my little darling a big teddy bear.

In an instant, the hero in her little eyes is no longer daddy, but some strange, young creep.

I tell you, a midway makes me want to sit down and cry.

The physician's office fun run

Mother Nature has human development all screwed up.

She did it intentionally as a cruel joke on fathers, sort of retribution for their not having to go through pregnancy.

You see, nature has given babies the ability to move before they acquire reason.

If it were up to me to develop little humans, I'd turn that order around.

But, nature always sides with the kids.

Look at it from the kid's perspective.

For the better part of nine months you're locked up in a womb with absolutely nothing to do.

You can't see, and even if you could, there wouldn't be anything really exciting to look at. That's one place on Earth they can't put a television.

You can't hear anything except an occasional gurgling when mommy gets indigestion.

So, you're sitting there saying to yourself, "If I ever get out of here, nobody is every going to pen me up like this again."

All of a sudden, boom you're born. Whoopie! Freedom at last.

Unfortunately you can't move. For the better part of a year and a half you are totally frustrated. Here is this grand and glorious world to explore, and you can't go anywhere except where your parents carry you. And, they never go anyplace interesting.

Finally you learn to crawl, then walk and eventually run. Suddenly the world becomes one giant playground. Never mind that you don't have the intelligence to understand it. Heck, you don't have to understand something to enjoy it.

All this leads up to the following tale of parental woe.

I was at the doctor's office the other day. My wife had volunteered my services to watch the kid while she saw her physician. No sweat, I told myself as I took the kid from her.

Well, the instant I set that kid down, she took off down the waiting room aisle like Carl Lewis running the 100 yard dash.

"Come back here you little rugrat!" I yelled as a couple of women gave me nasty looks.

Like Edwin Moses, I hurdled several rows of chairs in an attempt to catch the little traveler. Except the kid turned the other way and disappeared into the clinic's accounting office.

Seconds later there came a horrible shriek. I peeked in the office door and saw my kid underneath a desk, grabbing the kneecaps of a very, very startled secretary.

When she spotted me, the kid ran out from under the desk, climbed a chair onto another desk and proceeded to send papers flying with her arms and legs. I snatched the kid up and whisked her back into the waiting room.

I put the kid in a chair, but before you could say "sit there" she was once again running down the waiting room aisle, this time disappearing down the hall leading to the doctors' offices.

I lost her in a hallway of closed doors. She had me. Hey, no way was I going to go looking for my kid behind those doors. I could just see myself opening the first door and encountering a half naked lady.

"Don't worry ma'am, I'm, uh, a genealogy-obstructitian intern," I'd stammer.

"Pervert!" She would scream.

My mind snapped back to reality when I heard a crashing sound coming from an open doorway. I raced down the hall and discovered my kid in an empty examination room gleefully cleaning off the last of three shelves of tissues, tongue depressors and once sterile medical instruments.

Just then the doctor walked in. He looked at the examination table where the kid had just pulled the paper covering off the table. It lay on the floor like a huge unraveled roll of toilet paper.

He smiled at the kid, patted her on the head, and then gave me a look which told me I'd better take out a second mortgage on my house if I expected to pay my wife's doctor bill.

Well, I just stood there watching my kid chew on a tongue depressor and listened to Mother Nature laughing.

Chapter Three

Car seats are pure torture

Car seats are great for child safety, pure torture for parents.

Don't get me wrong, they should be used to prevent a child from becoming seriously injured in an accident. But, boy, do they exact a price.

Because of car seats, pleasant rides in the country are a thing of the past for my wife and I.

Recently my wife, the kid and I traveled to Tomah, about a two hour drive from Wausau.

Ten minutes into the trip the kid began squirming and screaming in her padded seat.

And, she made it perfectly clear that so long as she was forced to sit in that car seat she would make like fingernails on a blackboard.

I was thankful the windows were rolled up, else a passing motorist might think we were abusing the poor child when in reality it was the other way around

Nothing could get her to stop

She wouldn't take juice.

Give her a toy and she'd throw it back in your face.

I gave up trying to tell her to shut up. It's a concept not understood by an 18-month-old child. It is something they learn sometime between their 16th and 18th birthdays.

At one point I tuned the radio to a rock station and cranked the volume full blast. The kid merely increased her volume in response. Screaming and screeching in stereo isn't something a healthy adult can tolerate beyond a few seconds.

My wife seemed unconcerned by the racket. She just calmly sat there looking out the window. I think women are born with the ability to tune out crying kids. It's sort of compensation for nature putting them through the rigors of childbirth.

Meanwhile I was hunched over the wheel, my hands welded to it by taut nerves. I looked and felt like I had just consumed a dozen cups of coffee.

An interesting thing occurs when a father reaches that point.

It seems the more the kid screams, the harder the father's foot presses against the accelerator. Without him realizing it, the car speeds up.

Well, before I knew it, we were doing 85.

Then I had two people screaming at me. My wife was yelling at me for failing to observe safe driving speeds, and my kid was screaming because she was confined.

I glanced in my rear view mirror and saw only flashes of blue and red light.

"I wonder if he'll accept a plea of insanity," I said to my wife as my head fell against the steering wheel.

The kid started screaming louder. She does that because the only thing she hates worse than being in a car seat in a moving car is being in a car seat in a parked car.

The officer walked up to the open window.

"Could I see you.. ma'am does your husband always bite the steering wheel like that?"

I slowly removed my mouth from the steering wheel and smiled meekly.

"You on drugs, mister or what?" the officer said sternly.

"I wish, I wish," I replied. "I mean, can't you hear my kid crying in the back."

"Crying? I don't hear any crying," the officer said. I whipped around and discovered my kid was fast asleep in her seat.

The officer gave me the ticket and drove off. Before the tires of my car hit pavement, the kid was awake and screaming. This time my wife was screaming with her.

I am convinced the vocal cords of a baby are stronger by far than the adult eardrum because by the time we reached Tomah I was deaf and the kid was still crying.

It took me three beers to settle down from the drive.

About the fourth beer, I got to wondering if it would be legal to strap the kid and the car seat to the rooftop carrier.

Color my walls

They say that a pen in the hands of a journalist is a dangerous thing.

Well, a journalist is a wimp compared to a 22-month-old kid armed with a Crayola crayon.

I don't know what makes parents torture themselves so, but they do, day in and day out. Like when they think their pride and joy is ready to express herself artistically.

"Isn't that cute," my wife says to me as we watch our daughter draw erratic lines on a piece of blank scratch paper.

And for a moment we entertain visions that this newfound talent might occupy the little terror so mommy and daddy won't have to watch her every second of the day.

I tell you parents must take dumb pills every morning.

How else could you explain how we came to leave that little carpet creeper alone in the living room with a full box of Magic Marker Liquid Crayons?

We actually thought we were pretty darn smart.

I mean, for once in the Oakland household there was peace and quiet. We sat down at the kitchen table for what we thought might be a rare opportunity for uninterrupted conversation. The last time we had such a chance was when our daughter was 6 months old.

Alas, it wasn't to be.

One of the first things I learned as a parent, and it wasn't something I had read in a book, is that when a small child is quiet, he or she is up to no good.

It's nature's early warning system.

As my wife and I talked, I gradually became aware that I wasn't hearing any sounds coming from the living room. Not a giggle, a squeal, cry, burp, crash of glass or the thud of a toy being bounced off the living room table.

"I'd better go check on her," I told my wife as I got up.

"Donald, don't...don't spoil this precious moment together... the baby is fine...stay with me..." she pleaded.

"It will just be a ...Oh lordy!" Honey come look at what YOUR DAUGHTER has done!" I said collapsing against the doorway.

How can I describe it? Imagine, if you will, taking a half dozen garter snakes and dipping each in a different color of paint. Then taking a hundred millipedes and doing the same thing. Now picture throwing the whole works into your living room overnight.

"The kid is going to grow up to be a graffiti artist," I told my wife as she scanned the room desperately searching for the talented little tyke.

"There, behind the curtain," I said pointing to a moving bulge in the fabric.

My wife whipped open the curtain and then let out an anguished scream.

Our daughter, our pride and joy, our budding young artist, had covered the wall behind the curtain with purple marker.

I was amazed how much marking that kid did in 15 minutes. For a child who hasn't been walking for much over a year, her ability with a Crayon was awesome.

There were red squiggles across the TV screen.

There was blue ink tracked across the table my wife had so carefully refinished three summers ago.

Red ink was prominently displayed on the recliner rocker we bought new last year.

And, the kid herself was a sight. Imagine a punk rocker gone beserk in the lipstick section of the drug store.

She had red around her eyes and purple down her arms. Her blonde hair was streaked green. She looked like the victim of a child beating. For that reason we quickly closed the curtains, lest the neighbors get the wrong idea.

I guess a child psychologist would say: "Hey, this is all right, this is creative, this is a young mind learning to express itself."

That's easy for you to say, Mr. Child Psychologist. You don't have to clean up the mess.

Heck, have you ever tried to clean marking pen off the wall? Granite is less permanent.

Toddler curtails dad's reading and writing

I was once a fairly literate person.

There was a time I actually read books cover to cover; a time when I did more than skim through magazines or speed-read newspapers.

Believe it or not, there was a period in my life when I didn't own a television set. A time when I would come home from work, sit down in my easy chair and read.

And, I would write.

I would put a spiral notebook in my lap and begin writing something. Why, I once wrote an entire philosophy of life. It took 75 whole pages.

I wrote letters, lots of letters, thoughtful letters that were more than a "Hi how are you... I'm fine... the dog died, too bad... gotta go, promise to write again, Sincerely, Don."

Alas, those days of literature and letters are gone.

You see, I fell in love.

You can't read a magazine and court a girl at the same time. So, I turned my attention from pages to passion.
Then I got married.
Soon after I found time to read again. But, it had to come after I had mowed the lawn, paid the bills and cleaned the garage. Whenever I did manage to sneak a read, I was often accused of neglecting my wife.
There was little opportunity for serious writing.
Every time I'd get an idea for some profound essay, my wife would suggest I do the dishes, fix the bathroom sink or clean the basement.
Then we had a baby.
Babies don't care if you are well read or not. All you have to be able to do is change diapers and warm bottles.
Every time I'd pick up *Time* magazine to learn about what was happening in the world, the kid would start screaming for something. By the time I got done appeasing the little tyke, I'd be too tired to read.
It began taking three or four days to write a personal letter.
I'd sit down to write and get about four paragraphs typed before the little terrorist would start banging on her crib. I'd get up, take care of her, and forget about the letter until the next day.
Then the baby became a toddler.
Ever try reading something while in hot pursuit of a kid crawling across the living room floor? I tried it once. Walked into a wall.
My daughter doesn't understand how important it is for her parents to be aware of what is happening in the world. For all she cares the world can take a hike, daddy and mommy must devote themselves to her.
She won't let me read a newspaper.
When I get home from work, I like to plop into my easy chair and open up that day's issue of the *Daily Herald*. Before I'm through reading the first headline, my daughter is racing across the living room. Like an olympic broad jumper,

she hurls herself into the newspaper, crushing it into an unreadable ball on my lap.

Then she begins to play with the paper.

My kid is like a Cuisinart when it comes to anything paper.

I'd love to rent her out as a paper shredder.

My reward for trying to be an informed citizen is having to pick up pieces of newsprint scattered across the living room.

If I try to write, she bursts through the door and in an instant is banging away on the keys of my typewriter. She is like a concert pianist on speed.

I don't write personal letters anymore, I write apologies.

"Dear Aunt Minnie, I'm having a wonderful xitxwwLLpl.yoadfjlkajld... uh, please excuse this mess, my daughter just joined me."

One day I made the mistake of bringing home a best selling book. The next day I found it marked up with Crayon.

Nowadays, the closest I get to reading and writing is watching Sesame Street.

Swim class and other fatherly hazards

When a man decides he'd like to become a father, someone ought to take him aside and thoroughly explain what he's getting himself into.

Like, no one ever warned me about signing your kid up for swim class.

It's downright scary.

Like, you find yourself in this big room with hundreds of mothers who look as if they'd kill anybody who stood between them and the registration table.

Because classes are filled on a first come, first serve basis, you really feel the tension radiating from these women. Heck, I felt like a man trapped in a department store during a half-price sale.

It's high anxiety fatherhood at its best.

Like, I was sitting there in the fourth row waiting for the registration to begin and I was thinking about the 20 rows of mothers sitting impatiently behind me.

Would they riot if they saw the classes they wanted filling up?

I sat there imaging what that would be like. The image of a harried lady talking to a TV news crew came to mind.

"It was just awful, just awful. They announced Guppies I was filled and 75 women stood up and charged.

"And, I saw this poor man in the fourth row swept up by this massive wave of women... the next thing I knew, they had him pinned against the sign-up board, crushed against the Tadpole class list... he tried to cry out for help, but the women kept shoving registration cards into his open mouth."

Those cards worried me greatly.

You see, swim class sign-up is self-service. When you enter the room you are given these index cards onto which you are to indicate the class, day and time you want.

That made me very nervous because I never bothered looking at a class schedule. I relied solely on what my wife had written on a scrap of paper handed to me at breakfast.

"Now if you don't get this class, sign up for this one, and if you don't get that one, don't bother coming home," she said sternly.

What worried me was that I might incorrectly fill out the card. I could see getting up to the registration table, after an hour-long wait, and being told...

"Sir, I'm sorry but we don't have a Floundering Fish class at 10 a.m. Thursdays. I can't accept your card," says the teenage girl behind the table.

"But, but..."

"I'm sorry, but you'll have to fill out a new card, go to the end of the line and wait your turn..."

"But, my daughter's future and my life is at stake here..."

Suddenly I feel two hands on my shoulder. "Quit holding up the line!"

The next thing I know I'm being flung aside by two rather burly mothers. Instead of helping me up, the women just walk over my aching body to get to the registration tables.

But that would have been nothing compared to facing my wife.

"What do you mean you signed up for the 10 a.m. Wednesday class!"

"Isn't that what you wanted dear," I reply meekly

"I wanted 10 a.m. Thursday. No way do I have time to take her to swim class on Wednesdays. You'll just have to go back and sign her up for the Thursday class."

"Go back? And, face those mothers again?" I shuddered violently.

"See this bruise," I said pointing to my side. "I was just about to hand in my cards when this big momma leveled me with a body block."

"Donald! Did I marry a man or what! Go back there and sign up your child for the Thursday class. Make your daughter proud of you!"

I looked down at the kid and she looked up at me with a little smirk. I knew what it meant and turned to bid a hasty retreat, but my wife collared me just outside the kitchen door.

"But, before you go," she said with a sly smile. "Your daughter needs to be changed."

Halloween was a hoot the first time around

I wish toilet training was as easy as teaching a kid how to trick or treat.

Lately my wife and I have been struggling to teach our daughter that there is more to life than wet diapers. At the rate we're going, she'll be 14 before she's out of Pampers.

On the other hand, it seems the kid was born to trick or treat.

Last week I took my 2-year-old trick or treating for the first time in her life.

I figured I'd have a hard time showing her what's all involved in this annual candy orgy. She normally ignores my instructions.

Heck, she took to trick or treating like a 10-year-old.

It blew my mind.

I mean, here's a kid who can't even speak a full sentence conning an entire neighborhood out of a ton of candy.

I thought I would have to drag the kid up to the door and hold her against her will until she got her treat.

Boy, was I wrong.

At the first house we visited, I pointed my daughter toward the front door and gave her the bag.

"Okay kid, go for it," I said half expecting my words to be met with a blank stare.

Instead, the kid took a look around, saw what the other kids were doing and all of a sudden hiked off across the lawn.

Darned if she didn't march right up to the front door.

And, to my utter amazement she stood there, opened her bag and patiently waited for the candy to fall. Then she turned around and joined other children in attacking the next house.

"It's herd instinct," a fellow father told me as we watched my daughter and three of his kids harvest candy bars from some middle aged momma.

Being so little, my daughter didn't have to worry about saying trick or treat, or a polite thank you. All she had to do was look up at someone with her big brown eyes and the candy just poured into her bag.

I don't think my daughter understood why she was doing what she was doing. I don't think she cared. She was getting candy, lots of candy, and that's all that mattered.

One problem was keeping my daughter from sampling what she was so effectively gathering.

I solved this problem in a most ingenious way, I thought. I reached into her bag and pulled out a sucker. Everytime she came back, I'd take her bag and give her the sucker in return.

That also solved a problem with the bag. I mistakenly gave her a grocery bag. After a few houses, it got so heavy she was dragging it down the sidewalk.

At one house my daughter didn't bother stopping at the door, but barged right into the house, walked across the living room and helped herself to a handful of candy in a bowl.

At that moment I was wishing I had worn a mask.

After that things went rather routinely, until we came to this one house. The door opened and behind it was this absolutely gorgeous redhead dressed in the sexiest witch's costume I'd ever seen.

I just stood there in awe.

When my daughter returned, I knelt down beside her, gave a couple of quick glances to see if anyone was nearby and said:

"Daughter, dear, I want you to go back to that house again. And, wear my hat so that the lady won't recognize you."

The kid gave me an odd look, but nevertheless complied. She went up to the house, the door opened and that same beautiful young woman appeared. I just stared as she gave my daughter another piece of candy.

We did this about six times, each time I altered my daughter's costume just slightly. I figured the lady might be getting suspicious, so I reluctantly took my daughter to the next house.

But, I'll always remember that one house where both dad and daughter got their Halloween treats.

Bringing home the bacon can be unbearable

Grocery shopping and small children don't mix.

For adults, a grocery store is where one goes to buy food. For a child, it's one big playground.

I tell you, taking a toddler grocery shopping is at best an adventure, at worst a nightmare.

When I first took my daughter to a grocery store, she was content to ride in the cart. Then she learned how to walk. After that she'd have nothing to do with the cart.

The next time I went to the store, I let my daughter walk alongside the cart. I turned my back on her once and she was gone.

After a frantic search, I found my little darling trying to pull the bottom out of a pyramid display of canned vegetables.

I reached her about the same time as did this wild-eyed store clerk. Had she managed to topple that stack of cans, I swear, the clerk would have killed me.

One time I lost my daughter in the produce section.

All of a sudden I heard a lady scream and the sound of a terrible crash.

Turned out my little terror had stolen a grapefruit and had thrown it like a bowling ball down the breakfast cereal aisle just as this grandmother type was reaching for her bran flakes.

When she stepped back, her foot landed right on top of the rolling grapefruit. Up went the box of bran; down went the lady. She probably would have broken her leg had she not fallen into a display of Cheerios.

The worst part of shopping with a small child is the checkout.

I never realized how nasty retailers are until I found myself battling my kid over a pack of gum.

I mean, there you are waiting to check out and your kid is eyeing up all these colorful packages of gum and candy.

"Gum," my daughter demands as she reaches for a pack of sugarless gum.

"We don't need any gum," I reply in a gentle voice.

"Gum," she repeats as she rips a whole carton of gum onto the floor.

"What do you want gum for, you don't even know how to chew it!" I yell as I pick up the packs.

"Gum!"

"No gum!"

Well, it isn't too long before the kid is throwing a temper tantrum while I am hurriedly throwing groceries onto the checkout counter.

As soon as I get all the groceries out of the cart, I sweep the kid into my arms to prevent any further pint-sized raids on the candy racks.

Have you ever tried to write out a check while holding a kicking, clawing, crying kid?

It can't be done.

Because of the growing line of impatient people behind me, I put the kid down so I can write out the check. She takes off like an Olympic sprinter and disappears.

Automatic doors are a real convenience except when you are in the company of a toddler. Such doors give them new found freedom.

I'm looking all over the store for the kid, and come to find out she has been on the sidewalk outside the store all the time. When I retrieve her, people glare at me like I just had abandoned the poor child.

I have this recurring nightmare that when I finally catch up to the little wanderer outside the store, I find the store manger next to her.

"You should be ashamed of yourself," he says sternly.

"Say what."

"Making such a cute little girl steal that pack of gum for you."

"What gum?"

"This gum," he says as he pulls a pack of Dentyne from the pocket in my daughter's bib overalls.

Nobody would ever believe my innocence.

I once thought grocery shopping with my wife was bad. Shopping with a toddler is 10 times worse.

Tiny terror tosses teddy

Boy, are small children fun to have around.

They do such cute things. Like what my daughter did to me the other day as we were taking a little drive down Highway 51.

I came up with the idea for the ride after my wife who had spent all day with the little terror, informed me in no uncertain terms that I was to babysit while she disappeared someplace to regain her sanity.

Anyway, we were toolin' down the four-lane when my daughter indicated she'd like to hold her favorite teddy bear. I handed her the bear figuring that if she didn't get what she wanted, she'd scream so loud the windows would crack.

All was right with the world. I was enjoying a relaxing drive and the little one was sitting next to me quietly playing with her Pooh Bear.

All of a sudden the little tyke let out with a shriek, turned and threw the teddy bear out the open window.

"Oh lordy!" I yelled as I whipped the car into a power turn that would have made the Knight Rider jealous. Judging from the awful screech and cloud of smoke, I figured I took two years off the life of my tires.

But it was a really impressive driving maneuver. Even my daughter thought it was neat. I could tell because she was laughing and clapping her hands.

However, not everyone shared our enthusiasm.

There was this lady in a Volkswagen Rabbit who had been behind us. She looked as if she had just seen death and was biting into the steering wheel as she zoomed past us.

Nor, was the driver of that 18-wheel semi truck happy. As he zoomed by he blew his air horn and made a gesture at me which I hoped my daughter hadn't seen.

Nor, was the state trooper happy. He was sitting in his car parked on the median strip a quarter mile down the highway. Before the dust even settled, he had his red and blue lights flashing and was charging up the highway toward me.

"Lovely!" I told the little terror, who seemed fascinated by the colored lights reflecting in the rear window.

Figuring the trooper would want some sort of explanation, I jumped out of the car, ran to the shoulder of the road and snatched up the bear. Trouble was the trooper figured I was trying to escape and drew his revolver.

"Freeze!" He commanded.

I whipped around. "Don't shoot, you'll kill the bear!" I shouted.

The trooper shook his head and then stared at the teddy bear in my arms. He slowly put away his gun.

He looked a bit shaken. I suspect he was expecting to confront a desperate criminal and found instead a grown man holding a teddy bear.

"What kind of drugs you on, man?" He asked nervously.

"Uh, you see, my daughter threw her bear out the window and I thought I'd just..."

"Make a U-turn on one of the busiest highways in the state. Are you crazy, you could have been killed!"

"Hey, there are some fates worse than death. Have you ever ridden in a car with a kid who just lost her favorite toy? It would be like sitting next to an air raid siren."

"Doesn't matter you violated the law," the trooper said.

"Officer, we're talking about a higher law here."

"Higher law?"

"A law which says: Thou shalt not deprive a child of her teddy bear. I mean, you just don't abandon bears on the highway...not in Wisconsin, at least."

"Well, I'm afraid Dr. Spock didn't write the traffic laws in this state. I'm going to have to give you a ticket."

He handed me the citation and I looked down at the fine. I about died.

"This is coming out of your allowance when you're old enough to get an allowance," I grumbled at the kid who was happily tearing a roap map to shreds.

Yes sir, children certainly make life interesting.

Napping and Sesame Street don't mix

Sesame Street really did a number on my mind the other day.

I've been watching Sesame Street lately because my daughter is usually watching it when I come home from work.

I like Sesame Street. In fact, I have more fun watching it than my kid does.

Then one day I fell asleep while Sesame Street was on. I recall I had just finished reading a *People* magazine article about Arnold Schwarzenegger when I dozed off...

I hear a voice with a deep Austrian accent coming from the TV. It's saying..."Let's party!"

I look up and there on the screen is Big Bird and this muscle-bound man wearing an olive green Army vest with grenades attached to it.

Suddenly Muppets dressed in camouflage fatigues pop out from everywhere. Some are holding M-16 rifles.

Big Bird pulls a Remington Model 110 autoloading shotgun from under one wing and hands it to the big man.

"What are we going to learn today, Arnie?" Big Bird asks

"How to count to seven," he growls as he turns toward the Sesame Street set.

He levels the shotgun at a small car parked in front of one of the buildings.

BLAM

"One," Arnie says with a sly smile.

He turns the big gun toward a streetlight.

BLAM

It explodes into glass dust.

"Two," all the Muppets yell

He turns toward a garbage can.... BLAM..."three..." BLAM, BLAM, BLAM, BLAM. In moments, the set is reduced to smoldering rubble.

"That was neat, Arnie, let's count to seven again." Big Bird says as the screen shows a slow motion replay of Arnie's gunplay.

Suddenly pretty Maria comes running out. "Big Bird, Big Bird! Guess who's coming?"

"Who Maria, who?" the big yellow bird says with much enthusiasm.

"Why it's Mr. Terminator!"

A red-eyed robot rises from the rubble with twin Uzi submachine guns in his metallic arms.

RAT TAT TAT TAT TAT TAT TAT TAT...

Muppets dive for cover as the bullets explode into tiny puffs of smoke. Oscar the Grouch pops up from a garbage can, unloads his .44 magnum revolver into Mr. Terminator's midsection and dives back inside the can as Mr. Terminator sprays the can with bullets.

Arnie and Maria walk over to the can.

"What is this?" Arnie asks as he points to a pattern of bullet holes.

"It's a square," she replies cheerily.

"And, how do we know it's a square, Big Bird?"

"Because the holes form four lines at right angles to each other," the bird says.

Suddenly Ernie the Muppet jumps up and tosses a grenade at a wall. The explosion creates a gaping hole.

"What's that, Arnie?" Ernie asks.

"Why, that's a circle because it's round," Arnie replies with a big grin.

The scene switches to a classroom. A teacher is giving Mr. Terminator an apple for being the most quiet student in class.

The camera focuses on one of his red eyes. Computer lettering appears next to it. "Appropriate response."

A. Stick it in your ear.
B. Gag me with a pipe wrench.
C. Go graze, you cow.,
D. Thank you, Miss Jones.

It was when line C started flashing that I awakened. I shook my head and vowed never, ever to take another nap during Sesame Street.

Parenthood, or why I am a prisoner in my own bathroom

I am a prisoner in my own home.

More and more I find myself hiding behind locked doors.

It is not because I've been a bad boy.

It's just that locking doors is the only way I can find privacy.

You see, my 2-year-old doesn't know the meaning of the word privacy. She doesn't understand that mommy and daddy have to be alone once in a while.

It's not that we don't love her and want to be with her. It is simply a matter of parental sanity. If parents and small children are confined in a small area for a period of time, more often than not, the children will end up driving the parents nuts.

Children don't understand adults have certain responsibilities and duties which they must perform alone.

Like paying bills.

The other day I was tackling a stack of bills and trying to save the family budget from annihilation. I was tapping out figures on the desk calculator like crazy.

I was in the process of balancing my checkbook when my overly mobile daughter burst into my basement office. I didn't notice her at first because I was concentrating on the six-foot long tape of checkbook entries, a list of numbers I had neglected to subtotal.

Just before I was to enter the last series of numbers, I saw this little hand shoot past my arm and land directly on the calculator keys.

A half hour of meticulous accounting went right down the toilet.

My kid loves keys.

If she is anywhere in the house, it is literally impossible for me to type a letter. As soon as she hears my typewriter clicking away, she is right next to me begging for a chance to pound away.

More letters to my mother have been ruined that way.

Our lack of privacy has been violated to such a degree that my wife and I have had to barricade ourselves in the bedroom to assure a good night's sleep. If we don't lock that door from the inside, sure as shooting into the bedroom will come that little bundle of boundless energy. She'll want: A. a glass of water; B. something to eat; C. the chance to bounce on the bed.

Once I made the mistake of telling the kid to go make breakfast herself. The next thing I remember is hearing a crash in the kitchen. I tell you, it really wakes you up seeing a refrigerator drenched in grape-apple juice.

There once was a time I could use the bathroom without locking the door behind me. Not anymore.

It never fails, the minute I close the door behind me, there comes a pounding from the other side. "Daddy, daddy, I want to go potty, too."

That's followed by my wife's frantic voice: "Donald! Let her in. She's got to go and we don't have another pair of training pants in the house."

"I don't care, a man's gotta do what a man's gotta do, and right now he's gotta do it alone," I yell back.

The pounding on the other side grows louder, but I don't want to give in because I feel privacy in the john is a sacred right. Anyway, I know the kid is bluffing. The only reason she wants in is to get into my wife's cosmetics.

Heck, if I have to chose between toilet and toddler, I'll choose the toilet everytime. It is far better to have a wet 2-year-old than an embarrassingly wet daddy.

Beets beat me at the dinner table

I never thought that after I got married I'd someday be arguing with a 2-year-old over the relative merits of the beet.

"Here try these," I told my little daughter, who had never experienced the purple vegetable before.

"Yeeeck," my wife grumbled from the other side of the table.

"Sssssh," I said, glaring at her. "I don't want you to bias her against beets. Just because you think they're disgusting, doesn't mean you should deny our children the experience of this most nutritious garden vegetable."

"Some experiences should be denied small children," she said under her breath.

My daughter looked at the beet on her plate, looked up at me, gave my wife a quick glance and then returned her attention to the purple vegetable.

"Come on, darlin, beets are good for you. Beets make you strong and healthy. Why, I bet Brooke Shields eats beets," I told the child who responded with a blank look.

"Donald, don't lie. Beets serve no purpose other than to gross out discriminating diners. You want nutrition, eat a carrot."

"Look dear, I knelt in mud this spring to plant beet seeds. I labored all summer pulling weeds so these beets might thrive. And, I watered them religiously so that they might grow plump and juicy..."

"Did I ask you to do that?"

"Uh, no."

"Did I ask you to plant carrots, squash, corn and onions."

"You did."

"And, did you?"

"I didn't. Heck, squash is too big, and my garden is too small for corn. And, I'd rather buy big onions at the store."

Our dialog did nothing to encourage our kid to try her first forkful of beets. I decided a more direct approach was needed. I popped one of my home grown beauties into my mouth.

"Mmmmmmmmmmm."

Then I turned to my daughter and said, "You know what is really neat about beets? They turn your tongue purple."

I stuck out my tongue like some rabid rock star. My daughter looked up in horror. "Uh, oh," I mumbled. " Me thinks me blew it."

"Darling, your tongue won't permanently turn purple," I pleaded. "I mean, for a kid who delights in covering herself with Crayon, multi-colored ink and any cosmetics she can get her mitts on, I would think she would find turning her tongue purple great fun."

Once again she gave me that blank stare before pushing away her plate of beets.

The following night, I gave my daughter a plate of cold beets, hardboiled eggs and beans neatly arranged in slices around a mound of mayonnaise.

"Dip the beet in the mayo and experience the taste sensation of your life," I told her.

Well, she dipped the beet all right, but for some reason I'll never know, she never put it in her mouth. Instead she just whipped the beet like a Frisbie onto the floor.

I gave up and ate the beets myself as my wife, who was laughing so hard it hurt, left the room.

To stop or not to stop

Recently the state Department of Transportation announced highway waysides will reopen.

Bless you DOT.

Having those stops will make life on the road more bearable for the Oakland family.

Anytime the family goes more than 20 miles from home, a fierce in-car conflict breaks out.

On one side is daddy, otherwise known as ol' Iron Bladder. He is legendary in his ability to go great distances without having to stop for a bathroom break.

Then there is his wife, who at the mere mention of something to drink feels the need for restroom facilities.

Finally there are the kids. Our kids do one of two things when they travel. They either wet or scream. Sometimes they do both simultaneously.

A trip to the grandparents' home in Appleton sounds something like this...

"Donald, can we stop," my wife pleads.

"Gee do we have to. Heck, we've only been on the road 90 minutes," I groan.

"WAAAAAAAAH!" the backseat contingent screams in glorious harmony.

"Honey, will you feed the baby and give the other one some more M&Ms. That usually shuts them up." I suggest as diplomatically as I can.

"Not until you stop."

"Stop where."

"Anywhere! What about the next gas station?"

Now you might think that is a reasonable request. Unfortunately, I hate to use service station restrooms. It's not that they are unclean. The reason is I feel guilty going to a gas station, using its facilities and not buying anything.

I have the same problem with restaurants. It's like: "Can I have a Big Mac to go and where's your men's room?"

The other problem is when you have a car full of family, you never ever get away from a restaurant with your wallet intact. Everybody is suddenly hungry.

An hour down the road and all that glorious consumption comes back to haunt you with frantic requests for another stop.

"No way," I say stubbornly.

"Donald, it's unhealthy," my wife replies.

"Hey, up in Canada I waited two hours because, baby, up there, rest stops are few and far between. So I walked a little funny when I got out of the car at that backwoods gas station. I survived. If I can do that, surely you can wait another 20 minutes until we get to your folks' home."

"It's not your bladder that concerns me, it's your brain," she fires back.

"Hey, look at the kids, they're all right."

"Donald! They have diapers on!"

"Come on honey be reasonable."

"REASONABLE! How can I be reasonable when my insides feel like I swallowed a helium balloon.!"

I look at my wife, I look at the kids in the backseat who have finally fallen asleep and I look at the service station ahead. Suddenly I'm faced with one of the hardest decisions a father has to make: If I stop, the kids will wake up screaming and won't stop screaming until we get to our destination. If I don't stop, my wife will start screaming and won't stop screaming until we get to our destination.

I tell you, a trip with the family is a study in stress management.

Did MTV rock my little girl to sleep?

I'm feeling terribly guilty.

I think I've turned on a new generation to rock and roll.

One night my eight-week-old daughter was putting up quite a fuss. I mean, nothing could quiet her.

I tried rocking her. I tried walking her. I tried feeding her.

I tried everything short of standing on my head and crying.

Nothing worked.

For a moment or two, I just plain gave up. I put the wailing kid in an infant seat, which happened to be in front of the TV, which happened to be tuned to MTV.

Suddenly the baby stopped crying.

I swear, except for the music coming out of the TV, the Oakland home was finally, peacefully quiet.

I looked down at the tiny little girl and saw her big blue eyes glued to the TV screen. On the screen was the rock group Asia and some strangely dressed young girl running through the rain.

The kid was fascinated by it all.

Another rock group came on and she watched that one, too. Nary a peep came from her tiny little mouth.

For a moment, I rejoiced for finding something to quiet the screaming child. Then, suddenly, I was overcome with a terrible feeling of dread. Had I doomed my second youngest child to a life of rock music?

Then I remembered a similar thing that had happen with my other daughter.

Sometime between her first and second year, I tried to get her interested in Sesame Street. I'll admit now I also tried to get her interested in TV in general, figuring it might act as sort of an electronic babysitter. I now see the error of my ways and I will swear on a stack of Spocks never to do it again.

Anyway, I couldn't get her interested in TV at all. I'd point her toward the TV and she'd just walk away.

Then one night I happened to be watching HBO when a music video came on. It was Tina Turner.

All of a sudden, the kid stopped what she was doing, walked over to the TV and watched Tina do her thing. Although my daughter hasn't shown much interest in MTV since that first encounter with video rock, she nevertheless continues to like listening and dancing to rock music on the stereo.

At times I feel as if I'm grooming the next generation of aerobic dance teachers.

Once I put a Barry Manilow record on the stereo to soothe my oldest daughter, but it just made her cry harder.

I was getting myself all upset when my wife came into the room. After I told her all my fears, she told me I needn't worry.

"My dad liked opera music and wanted both his kids to like opera music. So, while we were growing up, he'd constantly play opera music on the record player," my wife recalled.

"To this day, neither my brother nor I like opera."

Dining out is no longer peaceful

There was a time when my wife and I enjoyed eating out.

Then we ruined it by having kids.

Small children don't like restaurants. They don't understand a family restaurant means they're invited, too.

To them any restaurant is a maximum security prison. And, they spend the whole time trying to escape.

My eldest daughter refuses to allow me to enjoy a meal in a restaurant unless I consume all courses in under five minutes.

In order to attain some peace during dining, I have developed numerous strategies to keep the kids occupied while my wife and I wolf down our meal.

When my eldest daughter was little, I used to give her Cheerios, which she dearly loved.

Feeding her Cheerios one by one usually gave us 15 minutes of uninterrupted dining, sufficient time to devour the salad and meat portions of the meal.

I did find one problem with Cheerios. When she got tired of eating them, she would begin throwing them. She threw those little rings of oats like Frisbees.

The result was the kid made us look like a bunch of slobs. But, that wasn't half as bad as what happened when an unsuspecting waitress discovered Cheerios are as slippery as they are tasty.

You should have seen that waitress. Why she would have made Mary Lou Retton proud. Her backflip was awesome. However, when the tray of food she was carrying hit our table, it looked like someone had just nuked our meals.

After my eldest daughter had lost interest in eating, I gave the little one my key chain to play with.

Some parents try to feed their kids a different type of food. However, I've found it best to alternate food and toys.

In a pinch food can be used as a toy. At one Los Angeles restaurant, I gave my eldest daughter a small red potato to play with. She was barely a year old at the time. But, she loved it. She rolled it around her tray and tried sucking on it.

Suddenly she took the potato in her right hand and threw it over her shoulder.

The blasted spud hit the floor, rolled across the aisle and came to rest underneath the boot of a rather smartly dressed woman who was obviously trying to impress her boyfriend across the table.

Not liking to waste food, I got up and went to retrieve the errant tater.

Figuring there was no polite way I could ask the lady for my potato, I decided to steal it back.

I got down on my hands and knees and crawled under her table. Heck, that woman is so wrapped up with her beau, she'll never notice I was there, I told myself as I disappeared under the tablecloth.

Unfortunately, I grabbed her ankle instead of the potato next to it.

Up she went like a rocket. And, scream! Two waiters dropped their trays from fright.

"What are you DOING!" She yelled.

"Uh, my potato rolled..."

Suddenly I felt my body being lifted off the floor.

"Look you pervert!" her boyfriend said as he lifted me toward his angry face.

I looked toward my table for help, but it was empty. My wife had spirited the kid away to the restroom to avoid seeing her daddy demolished.

"Look, fellah, I'm no pervert, here's the potato." I held it about two inches from his eyes and hoped.

The guy gave me an odd look and then set me down. I stumbled back to my table and ordered a drink as the big man tried to calm down the distraught woman.

I told the waiter we'd like our dinner to go and asked for the check. He seemed thankful for both requests.

As I got up to leave, I could still hear that woman. She didn't believe the potato story and wanted the police called.

Obviously, the woman never had children or she would have understood what causes a man to do such things.

Dining out at the playground

Small children seem to blur the distinction between eating and playing.

Adults come to the table to enjoy a meal.

My kids come to the table to have fun and maybe, if the mood strikes them, have something to eat as well.

There was a time when my wife and I could converse at the dinner table. Today, conversation is somewhat limited.

"Why did you throw your peanut butter sandwich on the floor!" I ask my eldest daughter as my youngest daughter takes her right arm, lays it across her highchair table and then whips it to one side causing her entire meal to cascade over the edge like snow off a roof.

Both kids giggle.

I scold both of them, emphasizing that food is to be eaten not wasted. For my efforts, I have one daughter who has her arms crossed and is refusing to eat and another who is screaming her lungs out.

"Eat!" I tell my eldest daughter as my wife tries to comfort the 1-year-old.

"No!" The 3-year-old says defiantly.

"Look, either you eat or you go to your room."

"No!"

"Come on, try the pork chops, they're real tasty," I say as I try a different strategy.

"No!"

This negotiation continues at some length as does the screaming of the 1-year-old. Finally, negotiations break down and I must exercise my last option.

"OK, you're going into your room, right now!" I say as I get up and lift the little girl off her chair.

"No, daddy, I'll eat. I don't want to go into my room!" she pleads.

"OK, you can go back to the table if you promise you'll eat everything on your plate."

"I will daddy, I promise."

She returns to the table, takes a fork and eats one piece of pork chop. Then she starts playing with her peas, flicking them with her fork.

"Eat."

"I am eating, daddy."

"Well, eat faster."

Thus commences a new round of negotiations. My youngest daughter has finally stopped crying, but is now using her mash potatoes and gravy like fingerpaint. Soon her whole tray is covered with a layer of brown goop, as is her face and hands.

As I continue my negotiations with my eldest daughter, my wife gets up, grabs a washcloth and dish towel and attends to the mess on and around the high chair.

During the entire meal my wife and I have said only two words to each other and our meal has been interrupted so many times, I start feeling the burning of indigestion in my gut.

I suppose parents get used to this sort of thing at their home. But, when kids turn a restaurant table into their own personal funland, I start wondering if I'm cut out for parenting.

"My aren't we having fun," the man behind me says. I turn around and discover the man speaking is also the manager of the restaurant. He has a pained look on his face as he views our table.

In the center of the table is a huge pile of wet napkins, the result of my 3-year-old spilling her milk.

The floor beneath the table is covered with the french fries the eldest daughter threw at the youngest.

The youngest daughter has a combination of catsup and chocolate soft serve all over her face. And, half her meal is stuck to the front of her shirt.

She looks up and smiles at the manager. Then she takes her right arm, lays it across the tray of her highchair and whips it to the left sending her plate and all that remained on it onto the floor.

Meanwhile, my oldest daughter returns from the restroom.

"Daddy, guess what? I just went poop!" She says in a voice loud enough to be heard in our section of the restaurant. People at nearby tables suddenly stop eating. The manager rolls his eyes, lets out a long sigh and leaves.

"Look daddy, snow!"

"Huh?"

I turn around to discover my eldest daughter opening up those little packets of sugar and throwing the contents high into the air. I also notice people around us starting to leave or move to tables in other sections.

In fact, I thought I detected a collective sigh of relief when we departed that restaurant that evening.

Toddler's togs are a terrible torture

I'd like to wrap dirty diapers around the necks of people who design baby clothes.

Maybe it is because I'm a man who didn't grow up playing with dolls that I find it so difficult to dress my youngest daughter.

In my view getting a straightjacket on a raving maniac would be easier than dressing a 16-month-old toddler.

Why can't they make baby clothes with zippers that actually zip and buttons that actually button?

Why can't they put zippers in the front? Why do they hide button holes under the crotch?

Can you imagine a grown man having pants which button up the inseam? Yet, they make baby clothes which do exactly that.

It is hard enough to get my daughter into a pair of simple pants let alone trying to fasten two dozen snaps, three hooks and four buttons.

"But, it's so cute," my wife says every time I complain.

"Hey, the kid doesn't care if it's cute! All she cares about is if it's soft and warm. Heck, she doesn't even know she's a girl!"

"What are you suggesting, we dress her like a boy?" my wife replies with a hint of sarcasm.

"Yeah. I mean, why can't all kids younger than 2 be unisex? Just let them wear simple, easy to dress, sleepers all day. They're babies and sleepers are what babies wear. I see no reason why a child of 1 has to look like a pint-sized fashion model!"

"Sure," my wife says angrily. "If I weren't around, you'd probably dress both girls in burlap bags with clothesline for belts. What could be cheaper! And, dressing them would be a cinch. Just throw them into the bag and tie a square knot!"

"Be serious woman, burlap is too scratchy."

What my wife can't understand is that the American male has no prior experience when it comes to dressing small children. Heck, there were times in college, after a particularly grueling night of partying, I had trouble dressing myself in the morning.

I just think they ought to make baby clothes in such a way that I don't have to wrestle my daughter into her bedclothes.

First off, a child of 16 months does not sit still. It's only after I nearly put the kid into a half nelson that I get one leg of her sleeper on. Before I can get the second leg on, she has kicked off the first leg.

I have tried everything. I have laid the kid flat. I have stood her up on her feet. Once I even tried to dress her in the dark.

And, it seems like every one of her sleepers is a half size too small. I mean, it never fails that her hands get stuck halfway down the sleeves. While I'm trying to fish her hands out, making sure the fingers don't get stuck along the way, she promptly kicks off both legs of her sleeper.

After a half an hour, she is still in her diapers.

Finally I get the sleeper on. But as I wipe the sweat from my brow with an unused paper diaper, I notice that the t-shirt she is wearing is on backwards.

There are times when I get everything on her and then she decides to have a massive bowel movement. I won't go into gory details here, but suffice it to say, her actions require a total change of clothing.

So I plead with manufacturers of children's clothes: Keep it simple. Remember, in this liberated world there are men out there who are suffering with sleepers.

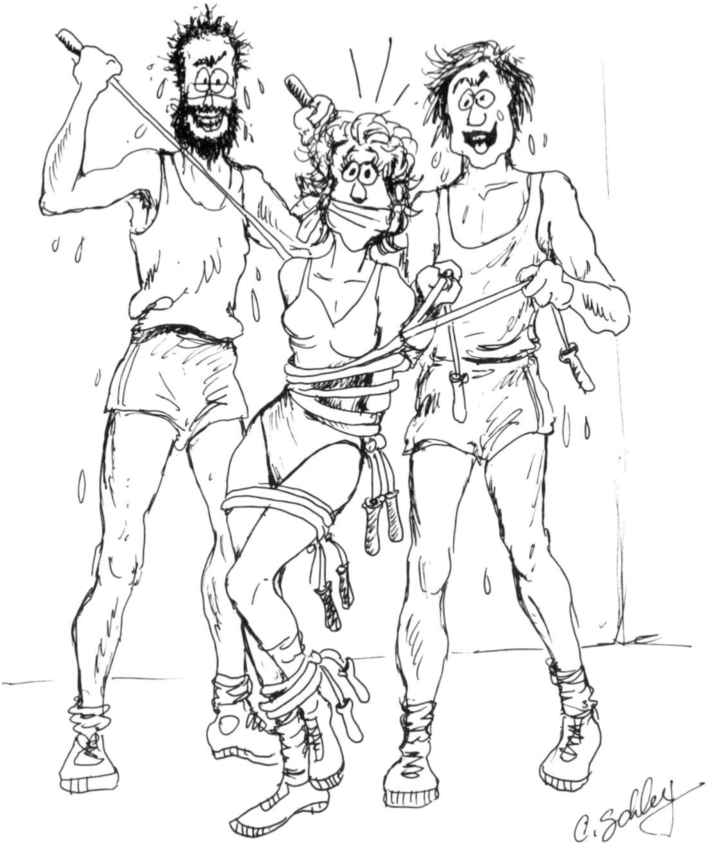
C. Schley

Chapter Four

Mutiny of the Aerobic

This is a story of obsession, passion, men driven to desperate acts and crimes upon the high gymnasium floors.

The Wildwoods Literary Society presents...

"Mutiny on the Aerobic."

The tall, lean man in the bright red sweatsuit with matching headband and hightops stood up and faced the judge.

"You sir are before this high court on charges that you led a mutiny of the 7:30 p.m. aerobics class and this heinous insurrection led to the captain of the class, Ms. Bligh, to be bound by plastic jump ropes, hoisted up and hung by her heels from a basketball hoop. Mr. Christian how do you plead?"

The man took off his headband and ran his fingers through his long, sweaty blonde hair. "Not guilty, your honor!"

Those in the courtroom gasped. Ms. Bligh leaned ahead of the prosecutor, turned toward Christian and cursed angrily: "May your soul rot in the belly of an old, smelly locker."

"Silence!" the judge yelled. "The court will now hear testimony from Mr. Christian as to the events which transpired that fateful night."

Christian jogged up to the witness box, leaped over the railing and landed in the seat. He put two fingers to his neck to check his pulse. He smiled and told the judge: "Well within my target zone."

"Oh get on with it man," the judge said testily.

"We were 12 weeks into the class. It was a long, hard session, but we didn't mind. We were a crew of seasoned aerobic exercisers used to the grind of choreographed calisthenics.

"The class of April 14 started out normally enough," Christian said as he toyed with the drawstring on his sweatpants. "There was no hint of the tragedy that lay ahead as we did our warmup stretches.

"As I recall we were midway through the abdominal strengthening exercises when we realized Bligh was doing something different. Instead of 10 belly busters, we were doing 15. And, instead of 10 leg raises, she had us doing 20.

"The men started grumbling as they held their painful tummies.

"It was when she switched from John Cougar Mellancamp to Huey Lewis during the side leg raises that I realized Bligh had gone off the deep end. The pace was too fast and the sets far too long for normal men to endure.

"It was obvious, Ms. Bligh had gone mad. Maybe she had her headband too tight, I don't know."

'LIAR!" Ms. Bligh screamed as she jumped on top of the prosecutor's table. "Just because I picked up the pace a bit you think me mad. You're all a bunch of sniveling sissies. Give you a workout, and you cry like babies..."

"You were KILLING US!" Mr. Christian yelled from the witness box. "We tried to tell you to slow down, but all you did was turn up the music.

"During the run around the gym you played heavy metal. It was terrible. My men were so exhausted they were slamming into the walls.

"You were no longer interested in fitness, but female domination of the male species. You had to be stopped, or we would all DIE!"

Christian tried to regain his composure by tying one of his shoelaces.

Then Mr. Christian continued by telling how his men suffered through one portion of the class.

"We were skipping around and jumping to the beat of KISS," Mr. Christian said. "Men were so exhausted they were tripping over their own feet.

"Still, Bligh would not relax the pace. I cried out to her 'Please, Ms. Bligh, a little Barry Manilow.'"

"'No pain, no gain, Fletcher Christian' was her response as she ordered the class into a marathon session of jumping jacks interspersed with hopscotches and knee-to-elbows,": Christian said with a pained look.

"My first mate in this class, Jacques Strappe, turned to me and said 'Fletcher, we must do something, that leotarded lunatic is going to be the death of us all'

"I turned to the red-faced man and agreed desperate action was needed. I knew well the consequences. I could be banished from the Y or, worse, lose my towel privileges for a year. But, I thought of my poor men, half of them lying on the gym floor clutching their chests as they fought off cardiac arrest.

"'Shall I bean her upside the head with my bean bag?' Jacques said to me as Bligh made us kick, twist, twist and kick... legs up, legs out, legs high, legs low, arms out, arms up, jump this way, jump that way...." Christian said almost hysterically.

"'Don't do it man, it's too dangerous,' I told Jacques. Anyway, no one in our class could throw a baseball two feet let alone a five-pound bean bag. I had a better plan which I whispered to Jacques and he in turn passed it on.

"We were all in the center of the gym with our jump ropes. Bligh, as usual was in the center of the circle. I yelled out the fateful command: 'Mellow Out Men.' Suddenly 10 men whipped their jump ropes over Bligh's head. Within moments she was bound tight.

"The men went crazy. They hoisted her overheated body up to a basketball hoop.

"I then led the men in a 10-minute cool down and we left as Bligh swung side to side."

The crowded courtroom erupted into a chorus of cheers and boos. The judge slammed down the gavel and announced he was about to render his verdict.

Bligh sat quietly in her lime green, full-body leotard. She nervously played with a coach's whistle.

"By the power vested in me by Jane Fonda's law of co-ed aerobics, I hereby find that Ms. Bligh did violate the code of fitness and did put her crew through an ordeal unprecedented in the annals of Jackie Sorenson.

"Bligh, I hereby sentence you to two years in the Vic Tanny Institute for Criminally Insane Aerobics Instructors and, furthermore, I revoke all your exercise privileges and confiscate all your aerobic cassette tapes." I

Bligh sat up, wrapped a white towel around her neck, did a couple of full body stretches and turned toward the courtroom spectators.

"Men today are such wimps!"

Jazzercise Japanese style

First there was aerobics.
Then came Jazzercise.
Want to know what the next fitness craze for women will be?
Boxercise.
Hey, take my word for it, it's coming out of Japan faster than a speeding Betamax.
The other day there arrived at my desk a Japanese magazine called *Intersect*. The cover story was about how Japanese folks cope with stress.
The article which caught my eye was titled "Punching Away Stress." Next to it was a picture of a Japanese woman taking right jabs at a punching bag.

It seems every Wednesday night a group of about 40 women gather at the neighborhood gym and spend about two hours whacking the ol' bag to the beat of jazz music.
"What is it about jazz boxing that has lured the traditionally shy Japanese housewife out of her home and into a gym, where she dons a training suit and gloves, spars with other housewives and works out on the big bag?" the article asked.
Well, if you ask me, I think it is the latent amazon in today's woman.
To heck with love and affection, women want the thrill of victory while watching the agony of a man's defeat.
I'm just glad I'm safe and married.
I can imagine what would happen if I tried to pick up one of today's women at a single's bar.
"Hi, can I buy you a drink?" I ask in my best Tom Selleck imitation.
"Beat it wimp face," she snarls.
"Uh, what's your sign? I'm a loveable Libra myself," I whisper.
"I'm warning you nerd, take a hike!"
Since the verbal approach isn't working, I try a little non-verbal interaction. I put my hand on her shoulder.
"That corks it creep," she growls.
"Bartender, 'Theme from Rocky'!" Moments later the jukebox blares that familiar movie soundtrack.
Suddenly the lady sends her right fist into my gut. I reel back as she catches my jaw with a left cross, then a right jab and another left cross. I bounce off the bar and rebound into a right uppercut.
Then she grabs the front of my shirt, lifts me up and sends me to the floor with a brutal right hook.
I try to crawl away but three other women, each bouncing and jabbing to the beat, block my way.
I try to stand up, but one of the gals chops me down with a combination right, left, right in perfect four-four time.

I look up at the gal I tried to pick up. She's sniffing loudly as she throws rapid fire jabs into the air.

"Come on, airhead, get up!" she yells at me.

"Come on I've got to go another two minutes before I achieve any aerobic benefits."

"Ah, he ain't going to get up," says one of her girlfriends. "Men are such noodles."

"You're right, Marge. Hey, bartender, a round for me and the gals. It's Miller Time," she says as she proudly rubs the knuckles of her right hand. "And, barkeep, take out the trash!"

She looks down at my bruised and battered body lying on the floor and laughs.

Something else worried me about this article from Japan. It was this sentence:

"There are even some daughters taking the course with their mothers-in-law."

Well, that would certainly add a new dimension to family relations.

What if my mother came over for a visit and made some critical remark about my wife's cooking? Do the two retire into the living room for a 10-rounder?

Can you imagine the fate of some poor slob who gets his mother and his wife mad at him at the same time? Heck, they'd wallpaper the living room with him.

For the sake of mankind everywhere, I hope the Japanese don't export this boxercise to America. I'd like to keep my teeth just a little longer.

And, now a little lesson in manners

The following essay contains strong parodistic humor and shouldn't be read by anyone who can't take a joke. This is only for those of you with a slightly warped sense of humor.

The following also requires this disclaimer:

The author does not condone any of what follows so you cat lovers out there don't write in suggesting I be lynched at sunrise. Although one of the most useless creatures on this earth, cats do have a right to live in peace and safety.

We strongly suggest that if you are a regular reader of the Wildwoods, you read the first "letter" and stop. If what you read turns you off, don't read any further as it only gets worse...

Etiquette seems in vogue these days as evidenced by the popularity of the Miss Manners column which appears in the local paper.

We thought the Wildwoods ought to take advantage of this fad and offer its readers--Mr. Manners, or the manly art of being polite.

Mr. Manners:

Our relatives are nice enough folk, but they visit us so much they are wearing out their welcome. How can we politely tell them to mooch off someone else? Signed: Privacy Please.

Dear Privacy Please:

We suggest mining your driveway. Watching their Volkswagen van disintegrate into a huge fireball is a subtle, yet effective way of communicating to your relatives your desire they visit a little less often. We should add that it is important to erect a sign at the head of your driveway that says the driveway is mined. That way, when Uncle Louie charges up demanding payment for his demolished van, you can say politely, "Well, didn't you see the sign?"

Mr Manners:

My 15-year-old son, Anthony, constantly slurps his soup at the dinner table. We have tried as graciously as we can to tell him that such a practice annoys us, yet he persists. Any advice? Signed: Grossed Out.

Dear Grossed Out:
Soup slurpers won't respond to a civil tongue. Soup slurpers are sick individuals who only respond to strong soup shock, which is accomplished in this manner: Go to your local bait shop and purchase one rather large and rather dead minnow. Pry open its mouth and stuff into it three, 1/8th ounce lead sinkers. Place the minnow in the slurper's soup, preferrably clam chowder. We guarantee his next slurp will be his last slurp-- and, the last time he'll ever eat soup again.

Dear Mr. Manners:
My neighbor has a cat which is constantly walking into my yard and scaring the birdies from my bird bath. How can I convey to my neighbor my objection to his cat's trespassing? Signed Catniption Fit.

Dear Catniption Fit:
Cat owners are generally unreasonable sorts not prone to accept any suggestion that the travels of their little darlings be in any way restricted. We suggest you deal with the situation one-on-one with the cat, i.e. 12 gauge No. 4 shot negotiation.
Such negotiations demand certain etiquette be observed and this varies from place to place. For example, in Western Marathon County, the proper sequence is to call out to your neighbor...
"Please remove your cat from my yard (10 second pause) BLAM!"
However, in Eastern Marathon County, the preferred etiquette is...
"BLAM! Please remove your cat from my yard."

Dear Mr. Manners:

My husband smokes a lot. How can I get him to quit? Signed: Coughing.

Dear Coughing:
Yelling at him is terribly impolite. Being judgmental is always rude. Be subtle. Rig a smoke detector above his easy chair. He'll either quit smoking or go deaf.

CPR class revives old college phobias

I had nearly forgotten what the agony of test trauma was like.

Why, the last time I had to take a test was in college some 13 years ago. After I somehow managed to get a diploma, I vowed I'd never take a test again.

Then my wife enrolled me in a CPR class a couple of weeks ago. She figured it was something we could do together and that it would be useful to know.

I reluctantly agreed to go on the condition that I could get home from the Tuesday night class in time to watch Remington Steele.

I also informed her that I would not do any mouth to mouth resuscitation unless the victim looked like Christie Brinkley.

It was only after I had arrived at class, that I learned we would be given both a written and a practical test, and that we would have to score better than 85 percent on the written test to pass.

Well, after hearing that I was ready to get up, go home and drown my anxiety in Old Milwaukee, but my wife had a grip on my arm that would have put a python to shame.

You see, I've never been much good when it came to passing life saving tests.

I started out OK when I aced the first aid test to get a Boy Scout merit badge.

Later I took junior lifesaving and flunked it twice.

The first time I failed because I couldn't get a 200 plus pound instructor off the bottom of the pool. Hey, I was a scrawny teenage kid and this guy was built like Moby Dick.

The second time I took the class, I figured I had it made because the instructor was an attractive young woman who couldn't have weighed more than 120 pounds.

I lived for the day I could fetch her body off the bottom. The trouble was I concentrated more on how she filled out a swimsuit than on studying the instruction book and consequently flunked the written test.

A boyhood dream of becoming a hotshot lifeguard swimming in girls drowned that day.

So, while the CPR instructor talked about heart attacks, I sat there thinking about how my wife had just set me up for a humiliating case of academic arrest.

The following week, we got to try out what we had learned on these dummies. My first go at it was awful. I stared down at this plastic person, who didn't look a thing like Christie Brinkley, and my mind went blank.

It blew my mind every time I had to yell into this dummy's face. "Annie, Annie are you all right? Someone go get help" One time I added "Preferably psychiatric help!"

My wife didn't have any trouble. She told the instructor she didn't have any problems working on the dummy because she lived with one.

The night before the big test, I was as nervous as a freshman at midterm. I set out to study for CPR the same way I studied for a Poly Sci final my senior year at college. I set out a box of NoDoz and a pot of coffee on the kitchen table and announced there would be no sleeping in the Oakland household that night.

My wife told me I was crazy and went to bed. Hey, some people study best under pressure and under the influence of massive doses of caffeine.

Well, that night I practiced CPR until I dropped.

I cardiopulmonary resuscitated chairs, pillows, even a Coke bottle. Hey, let me tell you, doing mouth to mouth on an empty 16-ounce Coke bottle at 3 in the morning is a real rush.

I even snuck into the room of one of my daughters and snatched the teddy bear from her arms. Boy, was I thankful no one was awake in the house to see me doing my "one-and, two-and, three-and" compressions on a stuffed animal

Heck, they would have locked me up for abusing Winnie-the-Pooh.

Well, I can report with pride both my wife and I passed the class. Good thing, too. Taking those tests probably took 10 years off the life of my cardiovascular system.

VCR brings royal discord

I fear the royal wedding of Prince Andrew and Sarah Ferguson may have caused some marital discord in this country

Consider, if you will, the following scene:

"My God woman, what have you done!" the husband screams with such force the neighbor across the street looks up as he mows his lawn.

"Did you say something dear," the wife says nonchalantly as she walks out of the kitchen.

"My tape, look what you have done to my tape!" he yells as he shakes a videocassette in her face.

"What tape?"

"My tape of 1986 Packer and Superbowl highlights, that's what tape. I found it in the VCR this morning and when I went to play it, instead of football there's some red-haired babe in a bridal dress."

"You mean Fergie."

"Fergie."

"Sarah Ferguson who this morning married Prince Andrew. You know the royal wedding in London..."

"Look, I don't care if she married King Kong, what in heck's name is she doing in the third quarter of the Bears-Patriots Super Bowl game?"

The wife gives a no-big-deal kind of sigh and proceeds to explain that TV coverage of the royal wedding started at 4:30 in the morning and there was no way she was going to get up to watch it. Instead she just grabbed what she thought was a blank tape, stuck it in the VCR and programmed the machine to turn on that morning.

"Well, why didn't you use one of your own tapes?" the husband asks. "Like one of those 'All My Children' tapes you own."

Suddenly the wife's face turns red and her eyes tighten.

"Touch one of my 'All My Children' tapes, just one, and you'll be walking with the homeless," she says wielding a metal spatula as if it were a Bowie knife.

"Okay, okay," the husband says as he takes his cassette tape and disappears into the den.

I suppose there could be other potential conflicts.

"Whadaya mean, you didn't program the VCR!" the wife screams from the kitchen

The husband sensing his wife is a tad bit upset, retreats into the living room. "I forgot," he says quietly.

"How could you forget! I must have told you a zillion times last night. In fact, I distinctly remember pushing you out of the bed and telling you to go do it."

"Well, I did, dear," the husband says as he continues to back away from his wife.

"I set the timer at 4:30 a.m.; I set the channel on NBC, and put in a blank tape... unfortunately, I forgot to push the programming button."

"How could you?"

"It was late and there was a baseball game on TV. I was about to hit the program button when someone hit a double with two on."

"What am I going to say when my friends ask 'Well, what did you think of the wedding?' Oh, I missed it because my JERK of a husband thinks BASEBALL is more important than me or HISTORY IN THE MAKING!"

At that point the wife throws up her hands and stomps back into the kitchen.

The husband plops into his easy chair and picks up the paper. On the front page is a picture of Prince Andrew and his bride. The man grumbles and quickly turns to the sports page.

Flu is definitely a weekday virus

Every so often it seems we are attacked by rampaging flu virus. Offices become deserted because everyone is home in bed. School children spread the flu like a Medieval plague.

As a public service, I would like to share with you, the Wildwoods All-purpose Flu Cure.

I just can't stand to see all you people out there being so miserable.

First off, this cure doesn't work with the stomach flu. If you've got that type of flu, you're on your own.

What I'm talking about is the flu which sneaks up on you like a cold, grabs you around the throat and holds you to the ground in a viral full nelson for several days.

The nice thing about the flu is that it gives you a license to be lazy.

If you want to get better, do nothing.

That's the first part of the Wildwoods cure.

As soon as you get the flu, go to bed and for the next 24 hours do absolutely nothing more strenuous than watch TV. And, if you do watch TV, don't watch anything that requires you to concentrate.

We recommend you watch nothing but MTV.

You'll start to feel better immediately knowing that you have suddenly been absolved of all life's responsibilities.

The flu is nice that way. I mean with a cold, people can still get you to do things. But, when you have the flu, nobody wants any part of you.

Now, some of you might be tempted to extend the first part of the Wildwoods cure for another 24 hours. That's fine so long as you aren't extending your illness into a weekend.

Nobody wants to be sick over a weekend.

So, that's why we devised the second part of the Wildwoods flu cure.

If you are still miserable as you head into Friday night, have your spouse go to the store and pick up the following items: A package of spinach, a half-gallon of vanilla ice cream, milk, chocolate sauce, a box of wheat germ, fish sticks and a bottle of 100 proof or stronger whiskey.

Okay, for supper eat the fish sticks and the spinach.

Fish is brain food. It will give your mind the little shot of energy it will need to direct the assault against the nasties in your body.

Spinach is the Roto-rooter of the human diet. A package of the green stuff will effectively clean out your plumbing from head to toe.

Your body will need extra energy in order to effectively battle those nasty flu germs. That means it will need a good dose of calories. And, what better way to provide those calories than a big, thick chocolate milkshake. Add a little wheat germ so the milkshake qualifies as a health drink rather than a dessert.

The ensuing battle between good cells and evil germs will create quite a ruckus in your system. So, just before going to bed have a shot or two of whiskey to help you sleep though the fierce battle within.

As you sleep, the good cells energized by the milkshake, will chase the flu germs out of your system and into the stomach where they will be flushed away by the raging spinach.

By morning you'll feel a little wobbly, but you will be free of the flu and ready to enjoy a much deserved weekend.

Use at your own risk

Nothing makes me seek the solitude of the Wildwoods faster than television commercials.

It seems producers of commercials go out of their way to be ridiculous. I guess they figure the more stupid they look, the better their product looks.

A while back I saw this commercial for a particular brand of toothpaste. This airline stewardess wasn't getting any dates. Then she used this toothpaste and in the next scene she is shown walking off the plane with a handsome pilot.

Aside from being a sad commentary on pilots (men who should be flying planes instead of noticing the whiteness of stewardesses' teeth), the commercial offered the suggestion that if you use this toothpaste, you will enjoy immediate success with the opposite sex.

After watching the commercial, I began thinking about what would happen if what the commercial suggested actually worked.

I envisioned myself walking down a department store aisle when suddenly this voluptuous blonde leaps out from the lingerie department and stops me cold with a flying tackle.

She begins kissing me passionately and holding me with the tenacity of a Lake Michigan leech.

"Your teeth, your teeth--- they're driving me wild. When you smiled just a minute ago, I knew you were the man of my dreams," she says, almost losing her breath.

All of this doesn't go unnoticed by my wife, who stands glaring at me from the ladies ready-to-wear.

"What's going on here?" my wife screams so loudly everyone in the store hears her.

"She likes my teeth..." I reply between kisses.

"Your what???"

"My teeth-- Must be that Pizazz toothpaste I tried this morning," I say, trying to wrestle out from the blonde's arms

"Honey, lay off my husband!" I see my wife grab the straps of her large purse with her right hand and watch as she draws it back in a wide swinging motion.

"LOOK OUT!"

I duck as that big purse flies over my head and slams like a wrecking ball into the blonde's puckered mouth. The woman tumbles backward through a display of brassieres and lands headfirst into a pile of foundation garments.

From out of nowhere, another strange woman appears and charges my wife like a pro football tackle. She lays a block against my wife that sends her reeling against a counter of perfume. Glass breaks everywhere and the air suddenly reeks of Chanel No. 5.

"Beat up on my sister, will ya," the woman screams at my wife.

The woman turns to me and smiles. "Hey, fellah, anybody ever tell you ya got nice teeth?"

My wife scrambles to her feet and grabs her purse.

"Ladies, PLEASE!" The store manager shouts.

POW!

My wife's purse scores again. Store clerks retreat and huddle around their manager, who lies face down in a pile of pantyhose.

I can hear police sirens in the distance.

"Time to go, little sister," the strange woman says to the blonde as she lifts the girl from the girdles.

"Uh, dear, we'd better get out of here," I whisper to my wife.

She turns to me and gives me a look that would frighten a guard dog.

"Ah, come on, honey. It was the toothpaste, I tell you--the..."

When I awaken I'm before the desk sergeant at the local police station. I can hear my wife arguing with someone about justifiable manslaughter.

"Can I help you, sir?" the sergeant asks.

"Uh, am I among the living?"

"We believe so."

"Boy, I'm never going to use that toothpaste again."

The sergeant smiles.

"If I were in your position, sir, I'd swear off blondes first..."

"You don't understand officer, it was the Pizazz toothpaste I used this morning."

The sergeant smiles again and laughs.

"I think your wife put an end to your brushing days."

Sure enough, all that was left in my mouth was tongue and gums.

How beer commercials should be

Beer commercials used to drive me to drink.

They don't anymore.

I enjoy watching them. In fact, often they are more entertaining than the television programs I'm watching.

I learned to enjoy these commercials by taking what the Madison Avenue types give me on the tube and applying it to real life, or life as I see it.

Here are three beer commercials Wildwoods style:

The scene is outside the biggest bank in the city. Suddenly shots are heard from inside. Three men burst out the doors firing handguns in every direction.

People dive for the ground as bullets shatter store windows and bounce off walls. The trio scrambles into a big black car which speeds off as a bank guard charges out of the building firing his revolver at the auto.

Police cars converge on the scene and take off after the car. A mad car chase ensues, with the black car skidding around corners, causing little old ladies to dive for sidewalks.

The car outruns each of the cop cars. The only one left misses a corner, rolls end-over-end into a pizza parlor. The big black car disappears down the street.

Everything is quiet. The black car is parked by a peaceful countryside brook, its occupants sitting on logs and counting stacks of money.

Soft music begins to play.

"It's Miller time," an announcer's voice says as we see one of the bank robbers carrying an open cooler of beer.

Here's another one.

"Let's go boys," the burly man says to his crew as they pile out of a pickup truck. Each man has a large coal shovel in his hands.

As inspirational, John Phillip Sousa type music plays, we see the men vigorously shoveling off the street piles of what appear to be clumps of dirt.

A series of tightly edited scenes flash on the screen: The men shoveling down Michigan Avenue in Chicago; on the Golden Gate Bridge in San Francisco; down Park Avenue in New York; a rural lane in Kentucky...

Gradually the camera moves back and we see the men are shoveling behind a large wagon-- a beer wagon-- a beer wagon pulled by a team of Clydesdales...

"For all you do, this Bud's for you..." a chorus of women sing.

One more.

You know those Michelob commercials that show this couple in front of a fireplace at some remote cabin. This guy and gal have just finished a gourmet meal and are relaxing and enjoying each other's company.

And, in their hands are long tapered glasses filled with chilled beer, presumably Michelob, poured to a perfect head.

An announcer chimes in with something to the effect that-- for such special moments--only Michelob will do.

Well, I think the commerical ends prematurely. Here's what they didn't show.

The front door bursts open. A woman rushes into the living room.

"Ah, ha! Caught you--you two-timing..."

"Omigosh, it's my wife," the man says with a voice of sheer panic. He scrambles to his feet.

"Business trip, my foot," the woman screams.

Sudsy drama could sell soap

I think advertisers are missing the boat by not mating soap operas with television commericals

Everybody hates commercials, but an awful lot of people love soap operas. By combining the two you could make commercials more palatable.

I mean, if Miller Lite and Stroh's can use humor to sell beer, why can't someone like Tide use sudsy drama to push laundry detergent?

Here's an example:

Two young women meet in a local laundromat.

"Sarah, I don't know what to do. Biff, my boyfriend, is seeing another girl. And, my mother just ran off with the meter reader. It couldn't have come at a worse time. Dad's getting out of prison Thursday.

"Sarah, you've got to help me," she pleads.

The other woman gives her a knowing smile.

"Mary, you shouldn't be using that detergent for your load of permanent press. Try Tide for cleaner clothes and brighter colors. Now, let me tell you the truth about Biff..."

As the camera focuses on Mary's shocked expression, organ music is heard. Then comes an announcer's voice: "Tune in tomorrow and learn Biff's terrible secret."

The following day the commerical begins with Biff putting a load of sport shirts into his top-loading washing machine. Suddenly Mary bursts through the door.

"Biff, my love, I know the truth. I know the real reason you've been going out with someone else."

"How could you?" he says in horror. "The only person who knew was my mother. Did she betray her only son?" he says as the camera studies his hurt expression.

"Well, your mother obviously didn't tell you how to wash clothes, Biff. You have to use Tide to bring out the color in those shirts."

"Really?"

Mary smiles. "Your mother didn't betray you, she just didn't want you to suffer alone. I know you were dating someone else only to save me the heartbreak of learning about your terminal illness..."

Organ music is heard as the camera fixes on Biff's pained expression. "Is Biff really terminally ill or is it a plot by Sarah to steal him away from Mary?" the announcer's voice says with a conspiratorial tone.

On the third day, the commercial is set in the detergent section of a grocery store. Biff is lowering a box of Tide off the shelf just as Sarah wheels up her shopping cart.

"You know," Biff says nonchalantly to Sarah, "this Tide is a far better buy than that liquid detergent."

Sarah looks around. "Biff, we can't go on meeting like this. I've got to talk with you."

"And, Tide really gets the stains out-- meet me in the dining room of the Hotel Despair at eight tonight-- with 14 active ingredients and no phosphate," Biff says, trying to look as if he is having an idle conversation with a stranger.

The two embrace in a passionate kiss right in front of the giant size Tide boxes. "Until tonight, my love," Sarah says breathlessly.

On the fourth day, we see Mary talking to her mother in the bus depot.

"You can't leave. Dad's coming home today," Mary pleads.

"He's scum, but I know you'll take good care of him. Remember, to get the grim out of those prison clothes, use Tide, there's nothing better," her mother replies.

"Before I leave, Mary, my love, I have to tell you. I was in the grocery store yesterday and I saw your best friend, Sarah, kissing Biff-- right there in front of the Tide!"

"Then it's true. Biff's terminal illness was meant to hide his affair with..." She begins sobbing. "And, to think I loaned my last box of Tide to that jerk."

Beauty only goop deep

I knew I'd get in trouble if I did it. But I did it anyway. I sneaked a peek at my wife's *Cosmopolitan* magazine.

I always get in trouble looking at such magazines because they upset my beliefs about womanhood.

Men should limit themselves to reading *Business Week*, *Field and Stream* and *Playboy* instead of reading stuff not intended for their eyes or sensibilities.

Anyway, I was reading *Cosmo* when I came upon a startling revelation on page 230.

When I view a pretty woman in a magazine--say in an advertisement for booze or cigarettes-- I'm not seeing a woman. I'm seeing powder and goop.

They say beauty is only skin deep. Let me tell you, it doesn't even get that far.

What *Cosmo* did was to photograph a model as she would appear without makeup. She looked pretty plain. Then through a series of 14 pictures it showed how she was transformed into an exotic and sexy model. You know the type--they're modeling blue jeans nowadays.

How'd they do it?

Goop and powder, as far as I can tell.

First she applied some Japanese creams (apparently the Japanese excel in things other than cars and cameras). Then she washed it off (I began muttering something about an apparent lack of logic in the actions of today's women). Then she applied some "bubblegum pink" cream and some brown contour cream to make her nose "chiseled."

Then she applied chocolate brown eye pencil, eyeliner, shadow, lavender powder, charcoal powder, pink blusher, cake rouge.

When she got to clamping her eyelashes, it was too much for me to bear. I threw the magazine aside.

To prepare myself to contemplate the implications of what I had learned, I went to the refrigerator and grabbed a bottle of beer.

It's all a lie, I told myself. And, man is the only creature on this earth who does this to himself.

I mean, when you see a beautifully colored bird, you see a bird with beautiful plumage. No bird dyes its feathers.

But, when I see the lovely Cheryl Tiegs, I'm not seeing the girl next door. I'm seeing the end product of multinational cosmetic corporations and a photographer's genius.

Look, a zebra doesn't go into a beauty parlor to get its striped mane streaked. So why should a woman?

Can you imagine some lioness sauntering up to a beauty shop and saying, "Please, make me a redhead."

Or a leopard saying: "Can't you do something about these ugly spots."

Don't get me wrong. I'm not against cosmetics for the enhancement of appearance. But, when they are used for wholesale change of appearance for reasons other than looks, we become actors, not humans.

Put another way, I don't mind if a turtle powders its nose. But, when it tries to look like a frog, I object.

If everybody plastered their faces with multi-colored gook just to look "beautiful," well, after the first rainstorm, we'd all have a rude awakening.

I figured that before I could solve this sociological problem, I'd better have another beer. However, in deference to my waistline, I decided to stay put and leave unresolved this burning question.

Color me Autumn

I heard something rather bizarre the other day.

My sister, who lives in Arlington, Virginia, told me the rage out there is to go to a color consultant.

For $70 this consultant will tell you what colors go best with your features.

I guess some colors tend to enhance a person while other colors seem to make a person fade into the woodwork.

With clothing, eating and now color consultants running around, you wonder how a person can make a decision on his own anymore.

I'd be a bit leery going to a color consultant. I could see the following occurring:

"Mr. Oakland, I suggest you remove that beard," says the smartly dressed woman.

"What!"

"Yes, it clashes terribly with your brown eyes."

"That beard and I go a long way back..."

"Well, if you must leave it on, try dyeing it a lighter shade."

The woman gives me an intense look, her eyes carefully scrutinizing every feature of my face. She gives me a sly smile.

"What color underwear do you wear?"

"Why do you want to know?"

"Tell me the color underwear you wear and I'll tell you more about yourself than even you know.

"Mostly white."

"Mostly?"

"Well, I do own a pair of lime green Monte Carlo briefs."

She gives me a disgusted look.

"Get rid of them."

"First you want me to get rid of my beard and now my shorts. I don't like where this conversation is headed.

The woman puts down her writing tablet.

"Relax, Mr. Oakland. To build a new colorful you, we have to start at the beginning, from briefs up, so to speak.

"Look, if you were in a car accident, they'd have to undress you, right? Well, if they found you wearing lime green Monte Carlo briefs-- well, they'd laugh so hard you'd probably bleed to death before they recovered their composure.

"Gee."

"Quite frankly, Mr. Oakland, colorwise you're a walking disaster."

"Gosh."

"But, it's not hopeless. I'm going to give you color charisma."

"Car iz ma?"

"You're an autumn, Mr. Oakland..."

"Because my hair is falling out?"

She smiles. "No silly, because of your skin tones, your hair, your eyes. You're an autumn and nothing can change it.

You either wear autumn colors or be a wimp for the rest of your life."

"You mean, I can't wear my new gray suit?"

"The only time I'd recommend you wear a gray suit is when you're resting in your casket. Only then would your skin tones blend with gray."

"How about green."

"It will make you look yukky."

"Yukky?"

"Look, remember that car accident I talked about. If you were wearing a nice tan suit, beige shirt with a monogram on the pocket and burgundy underwear, those doctors and nurses would treat you like royality because you were wearing your colors."

"No kidding?"

The woman folds her hands on her lap and smiles broadly.

"Look, I can't make you into a vibrant, dynamic person with grays, blues or greens. But, give me some browns, rusts and gentle reds and I'll make you commander of your own destiny."

"Wow!"

Labels--The stuff of dreams

The other morning while trying to convince myself the day was worth spending awake, I found myself in front of the dresser reading the back of my deodorant.

Have you ever read the back of a stick deodorant container?

"And I put that under my arms!" I said loudly enough to wake my wife from a deep sleep.

Take the first ingredient--propylene glycol.

First off, I have absolutely no idea what it is or what it does.

But, somebody thinks it's mighty important that it go under my arms.

Propylene glycol doesn't sound like it belongs in deodorant. It sounds more like a fuel additive for your car.

"Get 100 miles per gallon and clean you engine at the same time by putting in a quart of propylene glycol the next time you fill up," the TV announcer says as the camera shows high performance race cars ripping around a track.

"It's great for all makes of Japanese cars and makes a marvelous window solvent!"

The other thing that bothered me about propylene glycol is that seems to be related to material from which they fashion insulated underwear. I mean, is the stuff I smear in my pits a cousin of polypropylene underwear?

If that is the case, does that mean my underarms will stay warmer in winter?

The second ingredient in the deodorant is sodium stearate.

I like the sound of sodium stearate. It belongs in an Agatha Christie or Sir Arthur Conan Doyle mystery.

"Look, Holmes, a body!"

"Don't touch it Watson. Let me have a look..."

With magnifying glass in hand, Sherlock begins dictating what he observes as the good doctor takes notes.

"Notice, Watson, the tightly curled knuckles. Obviously the man was in great pain..."

Sherlock moves his lens over the mouth of the decease.

"Ah, ha! A trace of--hmmmmmm---I'd say Chablis, perhaps 1979, no earlier. And, what's this? Specks of white powder..."

"He was poisoned then?"

"Elementary, Watson, I deduce this man, not four hours ago while dining with friends, did sip from a glass of Chablis totally unaware that the innocuous carafe of wine was laced with sodium stearate.

"You don't say."

118

"Indeed! The chap enjoyed his meal of.." Holmes bends over the man's mouth and sniffs. "Beef burgundy, mashed potatoes and lightly buttered green peas. He left the meal feeling full, but otherwise comfortable.

"But, two hours later, he began feeling a slight pain in his stomach. Within minutes the pain was unbearable. Soon his heart succumbed to the stress."

"And, you say it was sodium stearate. The killer was ingenious."

"Yes, it takes a skillful chemist to produce the deadly powder. I dare say he was a medical man for how else would he have known exactly what dose to give to postpone the toxic reaction long enough for him to get well away--until he could get to a place where he'd have an irrefutable alibi, such as with the famous Sherlock Holmes!"

"What???"

"Yes, it was you who killed this man, Watson. I knew it the minute we met this evening. You had the smell of sodium stearate about you."

"Holmes, you ninny, that was my deodorant."

Etholxylated Mono--an easy choice

I've got to stop reading ingredients labels.

When I eat cereal in the morning, I almost always put the box in front of me and as I munch I read everything on it.

I have a particular interest in the crude fiber count. I mean, if they can refine everything else in cereal, why can't they polish up the fiber a bit?

I often wonder what non-nutritive dietary fiber is.

Maybe it's ground up memos and reports that once circulated among cereal company executives.

The other day while devouring an ice cream bar, I happened to glance at the ingredients label. I figured I'd find milk, sugar and ice listed.

Well, I found milk fat and non-fat milk. That didn't quite make sense. I mean, either you want the fat in there or you don't.

Reading further, I found ethoxylated mono and diglycerides.

Ethoxylated? Sounds like something that belongs in some horror movie, not in my Eskimo Pie.

Come on, did they really have to ethoxylate those glycerides? Why couldn't have they just stirred them?

To me, etholxylated summons to mind images of a mad scientist.

"Igor, come here," he calls to his hunched-back, pimple-faced, hairless assistant.

"I think I have found the secret of eternal life. One sip of this mixture and it's immortality!" the scientist proclaims as his assistant jumps and grunts with unabashed enthusiasm.

The scientist grabs two vials, each filled with liquid. "In my right hand, bachelor glyercides," he says with an evil laugh. "And, in my left hand diglycerides, the essences of all life!"

He pours the two liquids into a vial under the towering Telsa coils of a huge electrostatic generator. "Now, Igor!"

Igor throws a switch. A lightning bolt shoots from a shiny metal ball and strikes the vial. The scientist grabs the vial and drinks from it.

"Ah, nothing tastes sweeter than well-ethoxylated glycerides," he says with a sly smirk.

Suddenly claws grow from the tips of his fingers, hair spreads over his face and his mouth grows wide with tiger teeth. "Igor, what's happening?" he screams.

"Seems to me you undercooked your glycerides a bit," Igor scolds. "I told you to use the microwave!"

The other day I happened to read the label on the back of my wife's shampoo and found something called Balsam Canada.

Sounds like a good name for a new television star. I can hear the commercials for his new show:

"Move over, Tom Selleck, Balsam Canada is here."

Out walks a huge man with dark, curly hair, a thick mustache and a macho smile. He's wearing a heavy plaid shirt unbuttoned to expose thick chest hair.

"Balsam Canada!" the announcer says. "A roughneck lumberjack from the Canadian wilds who moonlights as a New York City private eye."

I can just see the opening scene of his series:

Out from the tall Canadian woods strides Balsam Canada. As he walks he unbuttons his shirt and takes it off, thereby exposing a well-muscled torso (swoon, girls, swoon). As he unbuckles his pants, he disappears behind a thick clump of bushes.

When he emerges he's dressed in a Saville Row tux. In one hand is a bottle of expensive wine. From the back door of his jet comes a gorgeous, slinky blonde... his gal Friday clutching a file containing his next case.

As their jet flies into the sunset, Canada and his secretary clink glasses and intimately discuss the merits of Chablis.

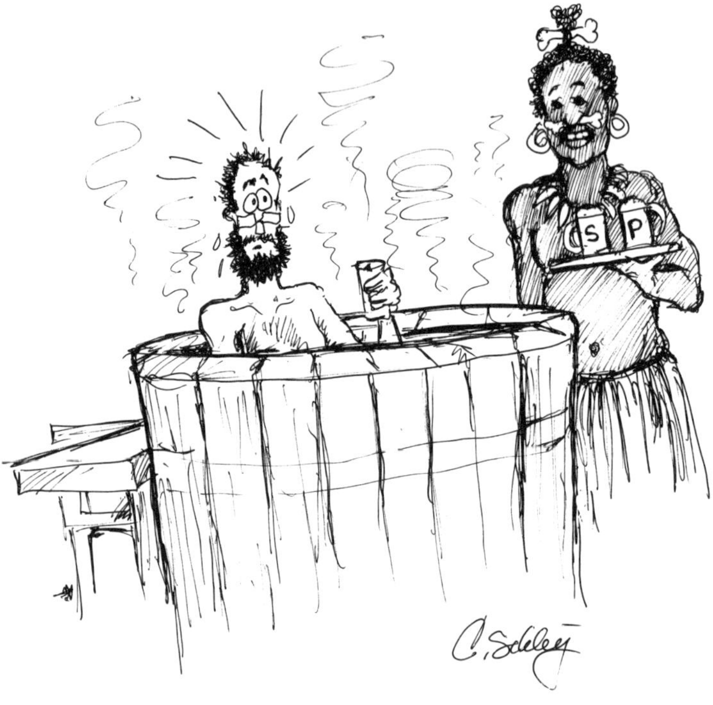
S
P

Chapter Five

Hot time in the ol' hot tub

"I've never been to a hot tub party before," I told my host as he escorted me out of the tub of wild waters.

Heck, how should I know it isn't polite to eat pretzels in a hot tub. Didn't bother me that the crumbs looked like guppies.

After I promised not to eat and soak, my host again allowed me to rejoin the party in the tub.

It was great sitting there drinking beer as the warm gurgling waters turned my body into something resembling silly putty.

I suspect that's why I accidentally dropped that full can of beer into the tepid tub, causing the others in the tub to scream and leap out.

It took the host and five of his friends about 30 minutes to filter out the bubbling brew.

After I promised not to drink and soak, my host again allowed me to rejoin the fluid frolic.

With great gusto, I rushed back to the tub, leaped into the air like the Karate Kid and entered the warm water in a perfect cannonball tuck. Once again the host hauled me out of the tub, this time scolding me for A) scaring the living heck out of those in the tub and B) getting half his guests and himself drenching wet.

After I promised not to jump and soak, my host again allowed me to rejoin the mini pool party.

After two hours of soaking, my body had assumed the color of rare steak; my skin had the look of a bloodhound's brow, and my brain had become thoroughly boiled. Like I was having these visions of Bo Derek rising from the bubbling waters as she did in the opening of one of her movies a few years back.

Suddenly, I looked up and there she was rising like some Greek goddess out of the bubbling waters. She beckoned me; I moved toward her and we embraced in a passionate kiss. For some reason I pulled away and looked over her shoulder. There was my wife holding over the water an electrical cord spitting sparks.

Passion suddenly succumbed to terror in the tub.

"I don't know how she got in here," I pleaded with my wife. "Well, I thought she was drowning, that's why I grabbed her... no dear, it wasn't a kiss, it was, uh, CPR, yeah, the poor girl was fighting for her life... whadaya mean so what?"

At that moment, I awoke from my daydream. Once again I was the only one in the tub. Seems the wild look in my eyes made everyone else nervous.

I was oblivious to it all as my thoughts turned from Bo to mayhem. I found myself considering filling the hot tub with bubble bath, and while my host was preoccupied with his erupting tub, sticking M-80s in the brats he was about to grill. Foam and fireworks, what a combination, I said to myself as I rubbed my waterlogged hands together and watched flakes of skin fall off into the water.

It was at that point my wife and two hefty gentlemen pulled my parboiled body from the tub, dragged it across the front lawn and rolled it into the trunk of my car.

I could hear my wife telling the host, "Yes, a hot tub can be a dangerous thing to those who have little experience with them."

My wife gains her personhood

Recently I was reading about an upcoming play when I came upon the word "personhood."

Personhood?

I looked it up in Webster's and it wasn't there.

Its context in the sentence was intriguing, but not definitive:

"It (the play) centers around a conflict between the macho man and the peace-loving doctor and the electricity of the wife who has recently discovered her personhood."

Electricity?

Gee, whatever personhood is, I hope it isn't contagious, I said to myself.

Then I began wondering what it would be like if my wife found her personhood...

"Dear, are you all right?" I ask my wife. "You look different."

"I am."

"You are?"

"Yes, I finally found my personhood!"

Suddenly the room fills with the sound of a celestial choir.

"Did you hear that?"

"What?"

"It sounded like the Morman Tabernacle Choir is in our cupboards."

My wife gives me an odd look.

She stands up and stretches her arms.

"I'm finally free-- free of the shackles of being a woman. I'm more than a woman."

""You've been reading *Cosmo* again. That's it, isn't it," I interrupt.

"I'm a person!"

Suddenly the room lights dim and the choir starts in with Gregorian chants.

"There goes that blasted choir again. Get outta my house!" I scream. I glance at my wife and gasp.

"Dear, you're glowing!"

"Yes, it's my personhood," she says solemnly. The choir starts up again.

"Ah, shaddup, already!" I try to regain my composure. "Dearest, why are you glowing?"

She smiles.

"The electricity of personhood flows through me."

"You telling me you're an eel or something?"

My wife puts two slices of bread in the toaster. She unplugs the cord and puts the end into her mouth. She pushes the knob down and the toaster begins browning the bread.

"Whoa!" I take a few steps backwards. "Hey, let's not go blowing any fuses, dear. Let's talk this out."

"There's nothing to discuss," she says, taking into her hands the cords to a coffeemaker and the refrigerator. Suddenly both switch on.

"I'm a person now!"

"Woman, you're the Weston III power plant."

"Her mood suddenly turns to anger. "You will treat me like the person I am!"

"OK, OK, but ease up, will you?" I plead, watching the bread blacken, the coffee explode from the pot and the refrigerator motor smoke.

"Geez, I don't know whether to call a doctor or an electrician," I cry out.

"Silly little man," she says with an evil laugh.

"Enough idle talk, it is time for you to begin work. I want you to fix supper, sweep the kitchen floor, do the laundry, vacuum the living room and clean the toilet.

"Woman, you're not only 120 volts, you're crazy!"

"She raises her right arm. A lightning bolt shoots from an outstretched finger and vaporizes a box of Fruit Loops.

"How would you like your hair curled?" she laughs as she hands me a broom and disappears out the door.

I shake my head and return to the real world. I resolve never to think about personhood again.

Mad city or the Twilight Zone revisited

Ever had the feeling you just made a wrong turn off Reality Road?

I experienced that weirdness a couple of weeks ago in Madison-- Wisconsin's bus stop to the bizarre.

It all began innocently enough. I happened to be in the big city one night and decided to catch a movie at a downtown theater. Trouble was I never checked the movie listings and arrived an hour early.

To kill time, I wandered up State Street. I forgot for the moment that State Street at night is the I-94 to Weird City.

As I walked toward the University of Wisconsin campus, I pushed against an uncoming flow of preppies, punkers, boom box break dancers and other less than conventional types.

The street was certainly alive that night. Suddenly I was overcome with a fear that everyone around me would erupt into some massive social upheavel, otherwise known as a State Street block party. If you can imagine what the movie Animal House would have been like if it had been directed by Federico Fellini, then you'd have some idea of what a State Street party is like.

Then for some inexplicable reason, everything became calm. It was as if somebody had flipped the switch cutting off the electric atmosphere enveloping the street that night.

I half expected to hear the voice of the late Rod Serling..

"Mr. Donald B. Oakland, a not-so-young reporter from a relatively All-American Wisconsin city, visiting Madison to catch a show, just strode past the bounds of the conventional and is about to take a front row seat in ...The Twilight Zone."

I found myself by a fountain near the State Historical Society. I sat down on one of the stone benches and looked around to get some bearings.

It was hot and humid in Madison. Yet, by the fountain, it was eerie and cool, as if air conditioned by a light breeze off Lake Mendota.

In front of the Memorial Library a group of young people formed a circle and began dancing to some weird foreign folk music. For a moment I thought I had stumbled onto the lusty pagan rites of a campus sorority.

Between the dancers and me flowed a parade of people: Hippie holdovers, jocks and alumni types in three-piece suits with "Hi, I'm..." tags pinned to the lapels of their coats.

There was a sailboat on the lawn of the Union. "Some skipper must have been on some heavy duty drugs to have navigated that feat," I said to myself.

It was then that I began to question the reality of what I was seeing.

I mean, all of a sudden two guys with fishing poles walked by. In Wausau it would have been a common sight. But in the middle of the University of Wisconsin on a Thursday night?

One carried a stringer of crappies, I think. I wondered if the two young men were bound for some dorm room to have a fish fry over a hot plate.

Across the fountain, sitting on a bench, was a lone man with long ragged hair and equally casual dress. He sat silently watching the dancers.

He bent over and reached into a cloth bag. From it he pulled a bell about the size of a fist. He held it up to his ear and with a pencil sized stick began tapping it.

The bell wasn't big enough to produce anything but a tinkling sound. I don't think anybody except me heard it.

He didn't seem to be dinging his bell to the beat of the dancers' music. It was as if he was sympathetic to the music, but unwilling to be bound by it.

I envied him.

I wished that I could toss off the responsibilities of family and job, rip off that uniform I wear to work each day, put on some ragged jeans, sit in some park and bang away at a little bell.

But, alas, should I actually try that, it would be a race between my boss trying to fire me and my wife trying to get me committed.

My attention shifted to my watch. It told me in no uncertain terms that if I didn't get my rear in gear, I'd miss my movie.

So, I bid goodbye to this Madison menagerie and raced back to reality: "Indiana Jones and the Temple of Doom."

A boy's dare, a sewer-searching experience

I grew up in Madison. My friends and I terrorized the Nakoma neighborhood during a time when the other side of the tracks was cow pasture.

One of the neatest things about growing up in that neighborhood was a storm sewer which split Chippewa Drive. It was a perfect playground.

Nowadays heavy bars make storm sewers inaccessible to kids. Good thing, too. Sewers aren't the safest of places.

But, when I was growing up there were no bars across the entrance to a tunnel which took the storm sewer underneath the street.

My friends and I always wondered what it would be like to walk through the tunnel, but none of us had the guts to do it. You could see daylight at the other end, but in between was nothing but blackness.

One day we were playing near the tunnel when Mark suggested we take a run through it.

He gave my best friend, Bobby, and me a stern look.

"Uh, uh," I said, shaking my head.

"Chicken," he said disgustedly.

See I knew what was in there. I watched a lot of television. Mark didn't. His family didn't feel television should be part of a household. Mark's bravery was merely due to ignorance, I told myself.

"There are spiders in there," I said pointing to a large cobweb.

"Nah," Mark replied.

"Big ones, too!" Their webs are like clothesline. They'll catch you around your neck and you'll never get free. I know, I saw it in a movie once.

"You'll be struggling and suddenly this spider as big as a basketball will come out of a hole and bite your head off. Then hundreds of its young will swarm out and have you for lunch."

"You're nuts, Oakland," Mark said as he laughed loudly. "Heck, I've seen older kids run through the tunnel all the time. Anyway, my mother has never said anything about spiders. I'm going. You coming?"

"Uh, what about the rats? I've heard rats as big as dogs live in there-- hundreds of them," Bobby said.

"Have you ever seen a rat around here?" Mark asked impatiently.

"Uh, no. But, I don't think I know what a rat looks like," Bobby admitted.

"You're both crazy. Are you coming or not?"

"OK," I said with a bit of hesitation. "Let's go!"

Mark turned around and disappeared into the tunnel. I couldn't see him, but I could hear him running. Bobby and I reluctantly followed.

We were about halfway in when a terrible scream echoed through the tunnel.

Terrified, we ran for the daylight ahead. It seemed like only a few seconds and we were out the other side. As we coughed and panted, we looked up and there was Mark on top of the tunnel. "Did you like my yell? Boy, what an echo," he said with a big smile.

In subsequent years, that tunnel became a refuge for us. If we had some secret stuff to talk about or just wanted to get away from our parents, the tunnel was our sanctuary.

One day I decided to explore alone another smaller storm sewer up the street. Unlike the tunnel, there was no light at the other end of this one.

With flashlight in hand, I began crawling into the black circle of concrete. It was damp and cold, yet I could see faint light ahead. Cobwebs tickled my neck and face as I crawled.

The light grew brighter so I turned off my flashlight. It was then I realized something was blocking part of the sewer. And, I began hearing a rustling sound.

Suddenly a match flared up and a man's face appeared. "HEY! GET OUTTA HERE, YOU LOUSY KID!"

I dropped the flashlight and spun around, crying and crawling my way back to daylight.

Years later I would realize what I had come upon that day was a teenager stealing a smoke. Nevertheless, the encounter put an end to my sewer explorations for good.

Just call me Amadeus

Just call me Amadeus Oakland.

Roll over Mozart, the kid is composing music like crazy.

Several weeks ago I bought myself one of those electronic keyboards at K mart and have been futzing with it ever since.

I've always had an interest in music composition, but I never pursued it because I lacked the discipline to learn to play an instrument or read music.

Hey, with one of these electronic marvels, you don't need to know notes. Darn things almost play themselves.

My philosophy on composing music is if it sounds good, it must be good music. Forget that major-minor, sharp-flat, key of G stuff. Play what feels good, I say.

I once had a chance to learn music.

I was in the fifth or sixth grade and my mother had enrolled me in piano lessons taught by this rather ancient lady who lived across town. Once a week I had to go to her apartment and play the most godawful stuff.

My favorite piece was "Volga Boatmen" because it expressed my attitude toward elementary piano theory.

But, you see, there was this dark-haired girl in class that I really had the hots for. I don't know if it was her looks that attracted me or the fact her father was a doctor.

Anyway, I much preferred pursuing her than practicing my piano lessons. Unfortunately, I never successfully conquered her affections or the piano's scales.

When I did sit down at the piano, I preferred to compose rather than mess with reading dull music. Composing is what I called it. Mother called it banging.

"Donald! Stop banging on the piano. You're upsetting the dog," she'd yell

I never wanted to play the piano. What I really wanted to do was learn to play the guitar. Seemed like guitar players attracted girls like crazy every time they strummed a chord.

Well, after less than a year I gave up piano, which probably made that little old lady's day. The absence of my errant fingers upon the keyboard probably added years to her life.

Except for singing in the shower or humming as I drive down the highway, I never returned to making music... until now.

Every night after the kids are asleep, I take my battery-powered keyboard into the bathroom. I close the toilet seat lid, sit down with a couple cans of beer to lubricate my creative juices and commence to play.

I prefer to play in the john because of the accoustics. It gives my stuff a real concert hall sound.

Sometimes I play soft and eerie. Other times I really crank 'er up. About then I start hearing from my wife.

"Will you shut that darn thing off and come out of the bathroom this instant!" she yells from the living room.

I lock the bathroom door and continue playing.

"Donald! I swear, I'm not going to answer the neighbor' telephone calls this time."

"I will not allow my creative drive to be stifled!" I cry out as I ram down a D minor chord, or something close to it.

"Look, if you want to be creative write something, at least that you can do quietly," she suggests.

"I'm a man of many talents, my dear!" I reply.

"Yeah, you have a talent for spending money on foolish toys, a talent for making a racket, and a talent for inciting riot among the neighbors!" she says sarcastically.

Suddenly my youngest daughter begins crying.

"Now you've done it!" My wife's voice suddenly sounds very angry. "With you making out like a screech owl in heat, she'll never go back to sleep."

"Oh, yeah," I reply defiantly. "Well, you just watch what happens when I start playing my lullaby allegro."

And, for the next 30 minutes, the kid and I make beautiful music together... until our concert abruptly ends with the ringing of the telephone.

Movie projector real test for Mr. Fixit

Movie projectors are a real pain.

You'd think that with all the technological advances we have achieved, somebody would have invented a foolproof projector that anyone could use without breaking into a cold sweat.

The trouble is you never use them enough to become familiar with their operation.

Oh, you know how to thread the film, plug them in or change a bulb. But, beyond that, most people are on risky ground.

Movie projectors hate teachers, particularly science and social studies teachers.

Back in high school, I remember one teacher who always seemed to get the oldest and most mechanically fragile projector in the whole school. He'd be all set to show the class some 20-minute movie and we'd be all set for a 20 minute nap when suddenly something would go wrong.

Like the time the soundtrack wasn't working. What came through the speakers sounded like a message from Mars.

Anyway, the teacher would spend the next 10 minutes trying to fix the problem. It was a no win proposition.

If he fixed it, then there wasn't enough time remaining class to show the film; if he didn't fix it, then he lost valuable class time and deprived us of our nap.

Movie projectors never fail unless they have an audience.

Ever notice the only time the projector at the cinema fails is when the theater is full?

And, heaven help the projectionist who can't fix the problem within two minutes. Longer than that, the crowd threatens to riot.

Movie projectors love to humiliate me.

The other night, I was at this class in which the instructor was going to show a movie. But, when she turned it on, the image on the screen was upside-down.

"Don't worry, I'll fix it," I said jumping up like some aging Boy Scout.

"Donald, sit down," my wife said under her breath.

"Don't worry dear, I used to fix these things in high school," I said as I flicked on the lights in the room.

Actually that was a bit of a fib. I always thought I could fix them in high school, but never had the guts to volunteer.

I gave the projector an analytical look and gave it a few hard pokes with one finger.

"Film's in backwards."

"We know that," my wife said with an embarrassed look.

"All you have to do is flip the reels and rewind it," I continued.

Judging from the fearful expression on the instructor's face, I got the feeling she didn't share my confidence. Nevertheless, I took the two reels off, reversed them and tried to put them back on. Except they wouldn't go on. I had forgotten that reels are made to fit on projectors only one way. It's a cruel joke makers of movie projectors play on the public.

"Well, that's easily solved," I said as I took a pencil from my pocket. I put the take-up reel on the projector, put the pencil through the reel with the film on it and held the whole works between my hands.

"OK, let er rip!"

The instructor put the projector in fast reverse. Within moments the reel in my hand was spinning like an airplane propellor. Suddenly the reel traveled down the pencil and clipped my thumbnail right off.

The next thing I knew, the reel was off the pencil and hitting the floor like the squealing tire of a dragster.

"After it!" I yelled as the reel shot across the room, bounced off a potted plant and careened down a hallway.

Film was shooting off faster than line off a reel on a pole held by a fisherman who just hooked into a Lake Michigan King Salmon.

As I watched the reel bounce down a flight of stairs, I turned to the instructor and said rather meekly.

"Oops."

Ol' salt croons into port alone.

One of the neat things about working for a newspaper is the mail that comes to your desk every day.

Like the day I got this newspaper from the Sea Heritage Foundation, Glen Oaks, N.Y. What caught my eye was the old clipper ships on the cover. Even though I was in the midst of meeting that day's deadline, I found myself compelled to investigate this nostalgic looking paper. I leaned back in my chair, put my feet up on the desk and started paging through the publication, ignoring for the moment the desperate calls from editors wondering where the heck my stories were for that day's edition.

The Sea Heritage newspaper, I discovered, is devoted to anything and everything about old ships, shipping, ship art, folklore and model building.

But, what intrigued me the most about the paper was the want ads. Some were like an old salt's version of the Dating Game.

"Female crewmate is desired to share the joys of Bermuda cruising with good looking, easy going 40-year-old man on 30-foot sloop."

Or "Seek lady with determination to sail across many horizons in fine vessel with seasoned captain with much to share."

Suddenly I found myself grabbing pen and paper...

"Bearded journalist who knows how to tie knots and doesn't get seasick except in high seas, seeks worthy captain to sail him away from his wife and kids for two months of exploring the Caribbean. Can cook and will give the captain the best journal ever penned upon the high seas."

I quickly threw the ad away realizing that my wife would have me walking the plank if I tried a stunt like that.

Along with the newspaper came a booklet of old sailor songs and a note that one could obtain a cassette of the X-Seamen from South Street Seaport, New York, singing these tunes.

I got on the phone to Bernie Klay, a former school maintenance engineer who publishes the Sea Heritage News and sings with the X-Seamen. After a brief chat, I ordered a cassette.

After that cassette arrived, my daily drive between Wausau and Merrill was never quite the same. Instead of tuning to a Top 40 radio station, I slapped Bernie's cassette into my tape player and joined him in singing songs of the high seas...

"Oh, what shall we do with a drunken sailor, what shall we do with a drunken sailor, what should we do with a drunken sailor... early in the morning," I sang as I navigated down Highway K bound for Port Wausau.

Sometimes I made up my own lyrics...

"Oh, what shall we do with a drunken reporter, what shall we do with a drunken reporter, what shall we do with a drunken reporter, early in the morning

"Oh, put him under the editor's desk, put him under the editor's desk, put him under the editor's desk early in the morning."

I tell you, driving became a whole new experience, an experience nobody cared to share with me. I started singing New York Girls Can't You Dance the Polka, and my wife threatened to jump out of the moving car.

My kids liked my singing so much they joined in. My wife said they were crying, but I said they were merely trying to harmonize with the ol' salt.

Practicing perfection is painful

The other day one of my co-workers was upset because she had gotten a traffic ticket.

A momentary lapse in concentration had cost her three points and a perfect driving record.

Although I sympathized with her loss, I told her I never had to worry about preserving a perfect driving record.

Two weeks after getting my license, I slammed my mother's car into another car. I said I never saw the other car coming. They said I failed to yield the right of way.

Then a couple months later, I backed into some woman's car in a grocery store parking lot. I said I never saw her coming. They said rear-view mirrors aren't put into cars for looks.

My first speeding ticket came when I was going to college. I had this Chevy with a big engine and four on the floor.

I was cruising up the interstate behind this dude going 80. I think the speed limit was 70 back then.

Anyway, in a moment of youthful dumbness, I decided to pass that car ahead of me.

The state trooper who had been following both of us didn't appreciate my bravado at all.

I think my record has been clean ever since -- more a case of not getting caught than careful driving.

Like the time I found myself going the wrong way on a one-way street in downtown Minneapolis. When I saw this line of cars coming at me, I did a truly impressive U-turn by jumping the curb and narrowly missing two parking meters.

Then there was the time I did a U-turn in the middle of Main Street in downtown Clintonville. Heck, the only place to park was on the other side of the street so I sort of took a shortcut to get to it. The Clintonville police officer who witnessed my perilous parking maneuver rewarded me with a warning ticket.

I tell you, I'm a traffic ticket waiting to be written.

Anyway, I got to thinking about perfect records and the last time I had a shot at one.

I think it was back in junior high school.

I had made it through one and a half years without one after-school detention. Then one day in an eighth grade social studies class, I got in one of those giggling moods. It was terrible. My friend was cracking jokes and I was in pain trying to hold back the laughter.

Well, it reached a point where if I looked at something, I'd start laughing inside. While the teacher lectured on something important, I had my eyes closed and my head buried in my folded arms on the desk.

Then the teacher, for reasons I can't recall, said the words "Hoover Dam." Well, the word dam literally broke the dam holding back all that laughter. All the class turned as little Donald Oakland laughed uncontrollably in the back of the room.

For that I got to stay after school.

In high school, I lasted two years without a detention. Then one beautiful spring day I got it in my head to skip school. This girl I knew had been skipping school regularly, and, as far as I could tell, never got caught doing it.

So I skipped school and what happened? The assistant principal happened to drive by just as I'm was walking down the sidewalk two blocks from school

The next morning my name was on the detention hit parade broadcast over the school's PA system.

A couple years ago, I thought I had written the perfect news story. Every name was spelled correctly. The facts were right. The grammar was all there. The story was interesting and read well.

I was so proud.

The next day the phone rang. The guy on the other end said I had spelled his name wrong.

You remember in the movie Indiana Jones and the Temple of Doom when that witch doctor ripped the heart from that poor devil? That's how I felt after hanging up.

I tell you, perfection can be hazardous to your health.

Oh, rats! Here comes another Oakland tale

When I'm at the table, after dinner conversation can border on the bizarre.

Like the other night when we sat drinking California Chablis and telling rat stories.

I find a good rat story is far more interesting than, say, a discussion of a USSR-US summit conference or high property taxes. A good rat story is like a scary ghost story told around the campfire in some desolate woods.

A little anxiety does wonders for digestion.

I started the conversation rolling, or should I say crawling...

"It was about 10 years ago. I was living alone in a mobile home next to a gas station in Clintonville. One night I thought I heard noises coming from the kitchen," I said in a hushed voice.

"I didn't think much about it until the next morning when I discovered some partially eaten pieces of bread on the kitchen table.

"'Mice,'" I said to myself. Then I noticed a half filled bag of bread had been moved about three feet along the kitchen counter.

"'No mouse could have done that,'" I said as I stepped back into the middle of the kitchen. "' I don't have mice, I've got rats!'" I screamed.

It got real quiet around the dinner table.

"Well, what did you do?" my mother-in-law asked.

"What could I do. I put out some traps and poison and waited... alone. I mean, nobody wanted to visit me anymore. I'd invited a girl over for supper, she'd spot one of the traps and when I told her what it was for, well, it was like firing a starter's gun for the 100 yard dash out the door."

"It was horrible. In the morning I'd awaken to the sound of rats ambling through the walls.

"Then one day, I went to get a pair of argyle socks in a drawer built into the wall and discovered where my uninvited guests had been calling home. They had made a nest in my socks!"

"How'd you get rid of them?" my father-in-law asked as he poured another glass of wine.

"Well, I had thought about staying up one night with a .22 in hand, but I cherished sleep too much. Eventually, the rats, two of them, succumbed to the poison."

"That's nothing," said Cindy, who comes from a farm family.

"You don't know true terror until you go one on one with a rat at the bottom of an empty silo," she said sounding like some old war veteran describing a fierce battle

"There we were, my mother and I, in this old abandoned silo when suddenly two rats leaped out at us. Ma grabbed a nearby pitchfork and started poking at the beasts.

"Let me tell you, rats are quick. And, jump! I swear there were times we were eyeball to eyeball with the ugly critters.

"Ma was pretty good with a pitchfork and our furry friends ended up as shish kebab.

"Then there was the time this family of rats snuck into the basement and took up residence in the laundry hamper. Ma couldn't understand why pa's shorts were suddenly developing holes.

"'Pa, whatcha ya doing out in the barn these days,'" Ma said holding up a pair of hole-filled shorts in front of the old man's face.

"Barn cat finally got the offenders," Cindy said nonchalantly.

My father-in-law put down his glass and lit a cigar.

"I don't have a rat story, but I recall one incident that happened one winter's morning. I was in the garage about to start my car. For some reason, I hit the windshield wiper button and up with the blades popped this rather large mouse.

"Well, it was quite a sight seeing this mouse cling to the moving blade. I shut off the wipers and sat staring at this mouse staring back at me. I quickly put the car into gear and when I pulled out onto the road, I made a hard, fast left.

"Sent that mouse flying," he said as he turned to the glass patio doors. "Sometimes I see him through these glass windows. He's standing there shaking his little claws at me."

Raiders of the lost panties

Spring makes me wish I were back in college.

I really miss the beer parties and panty raids.

That's what college in spring was all about. Studying could wait until midterms.

At the University of Wisconsin-River Falls, where I went to school, the first warm day of spring saw spring fever spread through the dorms like the flu.

Forget attending any classes after 8 a.m., there was serious party planning to do.

By noon, May Hall, the dorm I called home, would empty out as students raced to the nearest beer party. I'd usually end up leaning against a half barrel of beer buried in the cool waters of the Kinnickinnic River just outside River Falls.

It was life at its best.

No teachers, textbooks or tests.

We'd spend all day and half the night out there communing with nature.

Oh, we'd pay for our merry-making. The following morning could really be nice, yet it would be thundering and lightning between our ears.

You'd find yourself praying that you would recover before your first Monday class.

What we did at May Hall to cure our hangovers was to crawl outside a second floor window onto a small roof, lay down on a gym towel and bake under the noonday sun.

You tried to sweat the hangover out of your system before the sun fried your skin.

Another ritual of spring was the panty raid, a clandestine assault on a women's dormitory.

Whoever invented the panty raid had a warped sense of humor. Why anyone would risk explusion just for a feminine undergarment is beyond me.

I did it twice.

The first time I participated in a panty raid was my freshman year. It was a warm spring night and it seemed like the whole school body was outside. The conditions were perfect for little late night mischief making.

"PANTY RAID!"

That fateful cry sent a mass of men moving toward Hathorne Hall, a large dorm for women. It was also know affectionately as Hag Hall.

The next thing I remember, I was sitting on the shoulders of some big lunk trying to reach an open first floor window. I had absolutely no idea what I was doing up there, but I didn't care.

"Hurry up will you!" The big lunk yelled as my fingers curled against a window sill.

"Shhhhh!" I whispered back.

"Come on man... uh, oh... here comes the MAN!" I cried out.

Well, that big lunk took off like a sprinter, forgetting for the moment he had me on his shoulders. The next thing I remember, I was lying on my back in a bramble bush looking up at someone who looked like a college professor with rabies.

He told me something to the effect that if I would ever try something like this again I'd be academically emasculated.

Well, the second time I participated in a raid, I had matured considerably. I was a senior who had all my credits locked up.

A group of six May Hall marauders stormed McMillan Hall, a four-story girls dorm with maybe 300 women inside.

Through the front door we burst. Down the hall we ran screaming our heads off.

There was one problem. McMillan women weren't easily intimidated.

Somehow I got separated from the group and found myself face to face with this big gal ironing her skirt. Well, she jumped over the ironing board, and with that hot iron in hand, took after me like a warthog in heat.

I've never been much at track, but that night I ran like Jesse Owens. She was about to press the back of my skull, when I ducked into a room, leaped through an open window and flipped over one and a half times before hitting ground. I

144

was thankful I had sufficient beer in me to deaden the pain of the less than soft landing.

Yup, I really miss springtime at ol' River Falls.

Some sound advice from the Wildwoods

I now know what has been missing from my life.

I lack a soundtrack.

People should have theme music custom-made for their lifestyles.

I'm serious.

Watch any TV program. Nobody can function without music. Crockett and Tubbs can't do diddly without Jan Hammer.

Music gives those guys energy, a beat to live by.

I think my personal soundtrack should start out mellow. Waking up in the morning to Ozzy Osbourne somehow doesn't seem appropriate.

No, I think my day should begin with a soft little interlude by Liz Story or William Ackerman.

After I've had my Cheerios, then the beat can be picked up a bit with a touch of Whitney Houston or Elton John.

As I sit down to pound out my news stories, I think a more vigorous soundtrack is needed, something on the order of what Tina Turner did for Mad Max.

As daily deadlines near, something more raucous is required. Something to put me over the top. Something like the theme from "Rocky I."

Heck, the way I handle deadlines, Twisted Sister might be more appropriate.

After the deadlines are past, the mood calls for something weird, maybe eerie electronics from Tangerine Dream.

The soundtrack for the rest of the day could be drawn from Top 40, music just lively enough to keep the blood flowing.

On the way home, something uplifting is needed, something like the Mormon Tabernacle Choir doing the "Hallelujah Chorus." You make it through the workday, you have a right to rejoice!

To cool down at the end of the day, something slightly sentimental, like the themes from "Terms of Endearment" or "St. Elmo's Fire," would fit in nicely.

I tell you, nothing beats a well orchestrated life.

Nothing trivial about this pursuit

It was the wildest, wealthiest and roughest game the Wildwoods had ever seen.

If you didn't have $5,000 in your pocket, they wouldn't even let you in the front door.

I found the game in a remote backwoods cabin and knocked at the door. A small peephole opened.

"What's the password?" A surly voice asked.

"Trivial," I whispered as the door slowly opened.

A bridge party this ain't, I told myself as I glanced at the doorman, who had an Uzi submachine gun tucked under his shoulder. A gun like that could put 30 rounds into you in the time it takes to hiccup.

Inside there were about 20 men huddled around a large table where four men and a woman sat. I plopped myself into an empty chair and laid 50 $100 bills on the table.

The woman passed me a stack of chips as she took my money.

She was dressed in a low cut, cream colored satin gown. Long blonde curls wrapped around a face right out of Vogue. She had a body that would have made Hugh Hefner blush.

I was tempted to ask her name, but there were these two neanderthals behind her. They looked like they'd scramble your face if you gave the lady a second look.

"We're playing the Baby Boomer's Edition, can you handle that kid?" The man across the table growled.

"Try me," I said defiantly.

"What color you want, kid?" he asked as the light caught the deep scar which extended from his left eyebrow to halfway down his cheek.

"Green," I said lighting a cigarette. "And, a double Jack Daniels on the rocks."

He slid a die to me. I rolled a five and moved my green marker across the board to a blue square. I threw three chips into the pot and turned to the woman. She pulled a card from a box.

"What was the name of Wally Cleaver's best friend," she read in a voice so deep and sexy that I almost forgot the question.

I took a drag on the cigarette. "Eddie Haskel."

"The gentleman is correct," she said softly as she put the card away and turned her attention to the guy next to me.

I pulled six $50 chips out of the pot and passed the die to a funny little man with a pointy nose. Because of his nose and his habit of breathing through clenched teeth, they called him Weasel. He rolled a three which gave him a chance at a wedgie and big bucks.

Each wedgie entitled the player to one sixth of the pot in addition to whatever he had bet, if of course, he answered the question correctly. Weasel had two wedgies and a shot at one-third of the pot, about $1,500. If he guessed wrong he'd lose $500 for each wedgie and his bet.

"For a wedgie," the sexy lady purred. "What rock group is named after a celestial body?"

For a moment, Weasel stared at a man standing near the sexy lady. Then he smiled and said, "Bill Haley and the Comets!"

"CHEATER!" The scar faced man yelled as he pulled out a .44 magnum Smith and Wesson revolver and leveled it inches from Weasel's nose.

Weasel just smiled and watched as the end of a short barrel 12 guage shotgun brushed up against scarface's right ear. He laid the revolver on the table and the shotgun withdrew into the darkness.

"Shall we continue?" the sexy lady said coolly. The two goons behind her stuffed their 45s back under their coats.

The game continued for hours. At times the pot reached $50,000 with individual bets of $2,000 commonplace.

Weasel was eventually caught cheating on an Elvis Presley question. The two goons carried him out the door and that was the last anyone ever saw of Weasel.

It was 4 a.m. when I left the table. When the last card was read, I had $32,000 in my pocket. Nothing trival about that, I laughed as I walked out the door.

This baby boomer had done all right.

If you have the itch, scratch "Miami Lice"

At the start of every TV season, I find myself compelled to write to the networks. I send them letters containing ideas for new shows because the ones they choose to air are so bad.

Here's three additions to prime time TV brought to you by Wildwoods Productions.

"Miami Lice."

A jet black Datsun 280Z squeals around a corner and pulls up in front of a pastel colored elementary school in downtown Miami. The car brakes so hard it leaves a pair of skid marks a quarter-block long.

Out jump two tough, street-wise public health officers. One is dressed in a $500 Italian suit and the other in a pink T-shirt under a white linen suit.

Cautiously the men walk up to the front door of the school. A few steps inside they encounter a rather scuzzy looking first grader and slam him against a wall.

"OK, punk, where are they?"

"Where are what?" the kid says defiantly.

"Lice, man, lice! The place is crawling with them, and you know it. Now, do we talk here or do we take you downtown and give you a bath!" one of the men says as he lifts the kid up by his collar.

"OK, I'm cool. You want lice, check out that dude over there," the kid says pointing to a neatly dressed third grader. "He's a carrier, man."

The two men rip open their suit jackets exposing large aerosol cans held in shoulder holsters.

"FREEZE ... Miami Lice !" one of the officers yells.

The third grader tries to run, but the two officers tackle him in the hallway and bury him under a cloud of insecticide as the show's soundtrack blares Glenn Frey singing...

"I've got those body lice blues, baby...I'll be crawling back to youuuu."

***

"Hill Street Blue Jeans"

This is the story of an inner city pants store. Frank, the manager and head tailor, walks through the front door into a virtual madhouse of activity. People are everywhere and denim jeans fly through the air above them.

Suddenly there is a commotion by the changing rooms.

A clerk named Belker pushes aside two women looking at straight-leg jeans, jumps over a table of 501 Blues, crashes through a rack of cords and bursts into one of the changing rooms.

"Outta the store, lint face!" he screams at the young man inside.

"Get lost," the man scowls.

"GRRrrrr!"

Suddenly the clerk has the man by the neck and is dragging him out of the store. Next thing the young man knows he's flying through the front door heading for pavement.

"What is it, Mick?" Frank asks.

"Shoplifter. Caught him trying to switch jeans in the changing room. Grrrrr."

"Good job, Mick," Frank says proudly. "Here have a Milkbone."

***

"Di-nasty"

The scene is in Buckingham Palace, home of the powerful Windsor family. Princess Diana, the cold and calculating wife of the heir apparent, enters the room wearing a sexy miniskirt. The Queen mother bursts through the door.

"You're not wearing THAT in public!" the strong willed old woman yells.

"I bloody well will wear it!" the princess snaps back.

"I will not have all of England leering at your bony little knees," the Queen sniffs.

"Look prune puss, if you can wear those ridiculous hats in public, I can bloody well show a little leg. Anyway, Charlie dear thinks it's sexy."

"What does he know about sexy. He spends all day playing polo with the boys. We were once a proud family, a royal family; but, now we are nothing but fodder for those retched tabloids thanks to you."

"Oh, go lock yourself in the London Tower," Diana whines.

Nose news is not good news

There was a time when you could read a magazine and not have your sense of smell offended.

Nowadays you have magazines that you not only read, but smell.

What I'm talking about is this trend in advertising of putting scented ads between the pages.

I find this practice an affront to my sensory privacy.

Like I'm paging through my *Playboy* and all of a sudden my nose starts to twitch. The further I go into the magazine, the stronger this strange, sweet odor becomes. I soon recognize it is some sort of cologne and turn around to see if someone has entered the room.

Then I come upon this card advertising some hairy French cologne and a message which instructs me to pull back this fold to reveal the essence of a new fragrance.

I don't want to sample its essence. I mean, I'm already smothered by it.

And, I find it distasteful to be asked to interrupt my reading and to stick my nose between the pages.

Most of the time the cologne smells like it should carry EPA warning labels... "Don't use in a crowded room" or "Using more than two drops is a violation of federal clean air standards."

Reading a magazine should be an intellectual activity, not a struggle against nasal nausea.

Another problem is that the scent injected into advertising cards infects nearby pages. Even if you remove the card, the magazine still smells like some Yuppie dandy.

Worse yet, the card falls out and lands under the chair or a nearby table. For the next couple of days, you think some man is hiding under your furniture. Thank goodness we don't have any dogs in the Oakland household.

If this Madison Avenue trend proves successful, I can see other advertisers jumping on the scentwagon.

I can envision opening a copy of *Good Housekeeping* and being gassed by a sample of a new room deodorizer.

Or, reading a Betty Ford interview and being subjected to the essence of a new toilet bowl cleaner.

I could see this progressing to a point where advertisers compare their fragrances with products made by their competitors. Instead of a magazine, you'd have a bouquet.

Worse than that you could have...

"Is this how your bathroom smells..."

"Well, with new Beautiful Bathroom Air Freshner it could smell like this."

Thinking about this drives me absolutely paranoid.

I mean, the other night I reached the point where I was contemplating the idea of advertisers putting food scents into the pages of magazines.

Imagine you're reading *Good Housekeeping* and you come upon this ad for Gee Whiz Cheese Spread. You glance at the ad and turn the page. After turning the next page, your nose picks up a subtle fragrance. You stop to identify it. Your turn another page and suddenly you're aware the smell is cheese and crackers.

Suddenly you're thinking how nice it would be to have cheese and crackers while reading. And, didn't you just read about a new cheese spread...

I tell you, it goes beyond the protection of the First Amendment when I have to wear nose plugs in order to read my weekly news magazine.

TV viewing in half the time

Has television got you down?

Would you like to watch more TV, but just don't have the time?

Are teachers hassling you because you'd rather watch "Miami Vice" than study for an English test?

Well, the Wildwoods Academy can help you beat those tube blues with its new Learn At Home Speedviewing course.

Yes sir, in your own living room you can teach yourself to watch television two, three even five times faster.

You'll be able to amaze your friends by watching a half hour sitcom in just 15 minutes, and with full comprehension.

Imagine being able to sit through a 12-hour mini series in just four hours!

President Ronald Reagan uses speedviewing to watch entire episodes of "Dallas" reruns during breaks in cabinet meetings.

Felicity Nalebyter, a professor of economics at Georgetown University, watches entire episodes of "All My Children" between lectures.

You, too, can increase your viewing speed in just a few short lessons.

This course was developed by Wildwoods Academy researchers who were concerned about the negative impact television was having on students. It seemed if a student had a choice between a soap or a professor's lecture, he'd choose the former.

Knowing full well they couldn't make professors more interesting, researchers began studying ways to lessen the amount of television being watched by students.

This pioneering effort was perilous.

One researcher who watched no less than three hours of situation comedies every night, was found playing bullfighter with semi trucks on a freeway.

Another scientist who was assigned to watch non-stop Phil Donohue, suddenly developed hives everytime he heard a woman express an opinion.

Eventually researchers discovered there is a lot of air in TV.

Eliminate commericals, you cut a program's length 10 to 15 percent.

Eliminate the show's introduction and ending credits, you cut the show's length another 15 percent.

Researchers studying scripts determined that only about 10 percent of the dialog in a show was directly related to the plot.

With those findings in hand, researchers then devised a videotape player that allows the viewer to become ultraselective in what he watches.

Here's how Penelope Piston, a housewife from Peoria, Ill., is able to watch 20 hours of televison each week in just five hours.

Following Wildwoods Academy instructions, she programs her VCR to tape every show she normally watches during the week.

Then every Saturday night she plays that tape back at a speed 20 percent faster than normal. That's enough to hurry up the dialog without losing clarity. So what if J.R. sounds like Miss Ellie.

Next Penelope uses her five-speed, synchro-mesh, fast forward lever to race through all commercials, intros, credits and station breaks.

She also burns by any sex scenes because she has learned that they rarely make any contribution to the plot.

With bursts of fast forward, she skillfully edits dialog. After only a few short hours, she taught herself to recognize if a joke would be funny after hearing only the first half dozen words.

"Hey, if it ain't funny, it ain't worth seeing," Penelope says.

You, too, can be like Penelope. Just send a $999.99 bank money order...no checks please... to Wildwoods Academy and receive an 18-page instruction book, a high torque Korean VCR and three reels of high stress, non-break Pakistani FlexKing videotape.

Send your money today and get a complimentary copy of Speedviewer's Magazine. This month's feature is "Getting More Out of CBN and the Playboy Channel by Watching Them Simultaneously."

The ice cream personality test

Ever wish you could learn more about what makes a person tick without having to ask a lot of embarrassing questions?

Well, now you can.

The Wildwoods Academy School of Psychology and Advanced Plumbing present the Neapolitan Ice Cream Personality Profile Test.

The Wildwoods Academy is a prestigious learning center devoted to the study of science and fine arts, yet is an institution which believes its students should learn something useful as well. For every academic subject taken, a student must take a class in something practical, like auto repair.

One of our psychology doctoral candidates was fixing the float in a toilet at the home of the Dean of Fine Arts when the dean's wife came in and suggested he take a break.

To show her appreciation for the fine work he was doing, she gave him a dish of neapolitan ice cream.

However, instead of being scooped out, the ice cream was cut into a rectangular slice of strawberry, chocolate and vanilla flavors.

Suddenly inspiration hit. The young man dropped the dish of ice cream, and rushed out of the bathroom as the toilet erupted into something resembling Old Faithful

The young lad later hypothesized that the personality of a man or woman could be accurately determined by the way he or she eats neapolitan ice cream.

After extensive laboratory testing involving the consumption of no less than 150 quarts of ice cream, the graduate student wrote the personality profile test that would win him the coveted gold udder award from the dairy science and tractor repair school of the Wildwoods Academy.

This test is useful for men or women trying to evaluate people new to them, such as blind dates or prospective employees.

Here's how it works.

Invite the person to be evaluated to dinner. At the end of the meal offer the person a plate of neapolitan ice cream sliced so that each of the three flavors is of equal size.

Then sit back and watch how the person eats the dessert.

If he or she starts from the side, that person is indirect in solving problems, and is potentially a shifty person who is almost always unfaithful.

Those who start from the front or top are forthright and honest, real Boy Scouts. They'd be excellent employees, but not creative ones.

If a person tries to shape the ice cream into a rounded scoop, or if the person demands his ice cream be served in scoops, this individual is frivolous, impulsive, and chronically disorganized. For example, this person would make a lousy spouse, but a super lover.

If he eats one flavor at a time and takes extra care not to mix flavors, he is a meticulous person. He would likely be a Republican.

This type of man tends to love computers more than women; this type of woman tends to prefer housework to her husband.

If he charges in and eats the flavors indiscriminately, you've got yourself an overachiever, an aggressive win-at-all-costs type of personality. Anybody who gulps down ice cream is the type of person who shoots to the top of an organization and then dies of a heart attack at age 41.

If anyone eats the triple flavored dessert with a fork, they should be immediately referred for psychiatric counseling.

Our research found that people who ate the strawberry flavor first make the best lovers.

Those who ate the chocolate first considered themselves to be very macho or sexy, depending on the sex of the eater. However, they were also the people most likely to commit violent crimes.

Those who ate the vanilla first were wimps. Men who ate vanilla first also confessed to loving their mothers more than their fathers.

Women who eat vanilla first are the most sought after by men because they are very submissive, yet retain very aggressive sensuality.

Date those people at your own, extreme risk.

Chapter Six

That disposal could dispose of you, too

After five years of marriage, my wife finally got what she wanted: a garbage disposal.

I have been a relatively good provider for my wife, but I have never provided her that one modern convenience.

I'm a back-to-the-Earth kind of guy.

I believe in returning to the Earth what the Earth has given to me. So what if the rotting vegetables in the five gallon pail in one corner of the kitchen drew flies. At least if you kept the lid on tight, it didn't smell.

I mean, it's a crime to waste good compost.

After subtle coercion that only a wife can master, I consented to having a garbage disposal in the house.

However, I refused to buy it. I was gambling she wouldn't buy one for herself.

So, what did she do. She got her folks to buy her one for Christmas.

I swore I'd never install it. I warned her that I would probably electrocute myself while connecting it to a switch. Or worse, I'd accidentally turn on the machine at an inopportune moment. Should that occur, I instructed my wife to bury my remains in a mayonnaise jar.

So what did she do? She got her handyman father to install it.

I tell you, the woman is relentless.

One Saturday my father-in-law arrived with tools in hand. He took one look at the sink and said it could be a very tricky job.

"Well, I suppose if we can't squeeze it in there, we'll just have to take it back," I suggested.

"Nonsense, boy! We'll get it in, just might take awhile," he replied as he pulled a screwdriver out from his back pocket.

"Great! Give up the entire weekend to play plumber," I grumbled quietly as I passed him a pipewrench.

To my surprise we managed to make the electrical connections before noon and without frying ourselves with high voltage.

By 3 p.m. the monster was in place and growling.

I don't know why my father-in-law was smiling as he left that day. Was it because he had just scored some brownie points with his daughter, or was it that he had just stuck it to his one and only son-in-law.

I've never owned a garbage disposal. Consequently, the appliance and I endured a period of adjusting to one another.

It wasn't easy. Frankly, I didn't trust the darn thing.

Like one day when I fed it a couple of grapefruit. The machine started groaning and vibrating violently. Soon the whole kitchen was shaking. Dishes were jumping from the cupboard shelves and crashing all over the floor. It was terrible.

I thought at any moment that monster machine was going to burst through the cabinet doors and march right across the kitchen.

I envisioned the headline in the paper: "Man Mauled By Errant Garbage Disposal--Wausau Home Scene of Jaws IV"

Then there was the time I was washing dishes and accidentally let a steak knife slip down the drain.

When I turned on the disposal, that knife shot out of the sink like a Minuteman missile. The wicked thing missed my nose by an inch before embedding itself in the ceiling.

I have nightmares about that blasted disposal.

It's late one Friday night. I can't sleep so I get up to grab a beer. I grope for the light switch in the dark kitchen, but hit the disposal switch instead.

Suddenly the room is churning with tornado like winds emanating from the sink. The kitchen table lifts up and disappears into the sink's steel maw.

I struggle to free myself, but the suction is too great.

I brace my arms against the edge of the counter as my body is gradually pulled ever closer to the deep, dark drain.

Suddenly my arms give way and I...

Luckily I awaken before the inevitable and gruesome mauling begins.

Maybe some day I'll see how well the disposal handles a couple of M-80 firecrackers.

I mean, you've got to get it, before it gets you.

Pack ratting becomes an art

The other day while helping some friends move, I got to thinking about stuff.

I was carrying a hide-a-bed up a flight of stairs at the time and was listening to my bones and muscles make like Rice Krispies. You know: snap, crackle and pop.

I got to thinking that someone should make it illegal for pack rats to marry.

As I was straining to keep from dropping that massive piece of upholstered furniture on my foot, I began thinking about how much stuff my wife and I have accumulated during our six years of marriage.

I knew pretty accurately how much it was. It wasn't a week before I had decided to clean out the basement.

That is an event in the Oakland neighborhood. Come trash day the neighbors look with awe out their windows at the garbage trucks lined up like a National Guard convoy to haul away stuff from our basement.

Even after the garbage trucks have left, we still have wall to wall boxes filled to the lids with stuff.

George Carlin once described life as merely the collection of stuff... your stuff, her stuff, our stuff. As we progress through life, all we do is move our stuff from here to there. As we grow older the amount of stuff we move from here to there increases expotentially.

I confess both my wife and I are pack rats. Heaven help us if our children develop the trait. We will have to lease warehouse space.

A pack rat is someone who would rather sell his mother to the Arabs than throw away a high school annual.

And, a pack rat's excuse is always: "If I throw it away, sure as shooting I'll be needing it tomorrow."

At the Oakland household, we carry this to an extreme. I mean, I was going through a box and found themes my wife had written in high school.

I can't criticize her because I'm not any better. I'm just more efficient at hiding it. I still have short stories that I wrote back in seventh grade. And, I have saved every letter I have ever written.

I always say to myself that when I'm 60, I'll be able to sit back and read all this stuff. Of course, I'll probably not have the eyesight to read it.

Maybe I should put it in my will that I am to be buried with all my stuff so that I'll be able to read it into eternity. Of course, I doubt if the cemetery would like my casket being buried within a semi trailer full of junk.

Right now the only ones reading the stuff are silverfish. And, after they're done reading, they start eating.

It is hard for a pack rat to clean. I mean, every time I pick up something, I start getting all nostalgic. I remember all the fun I had as a kid and wonder how I managed to survive to adulthood.

By the time I relive my childhood, it's time to quit cleaning and have supper.

Pack rats cannot work together. Every time they pick something out of a box, they feel compelled to share its story with anybody within earshot. By the time they're done talking, they are too tired to continue cleaning.

The best a pack rat can ever hope for is to be organized enough to make more room for more stuff.

Spiders make house painting a hairy job

House painting is a royal pain.
I mean, it isn't the hard work, I expected that.
It's those spiders
The side of my house is a seething city of spiders.
Big ones, too. They look like snapping turtles.

I'm not kidding. I was busy scraping the west side of the house, right near the base of the chimney, when out popped this big, black eight-legged monster. Ripped the scraper right from my hands, he did.

I would have been a goner had I not had that hammer along. Took me a half an hour to scrape the remains of the critter off the clapboard siding.

Then there was the time I was standing on the topmost rung of the ladder, when a daddy longlegs scooted out from a crack and ran up my arm. It would have nailed me on the nose if I hadn't fallen off the ladder.

I woke up in a daze, looked up and there was that spider dangling from the crosspiece of the ladder and rappelling right toward my face.

Another time I was scrapping the trim when I felt a tickling on the side of my face. When I got down off the ladder, my wife asked me when I took up wearing earrings.

I ran to the mirror on my car and to my horror saw an angry spider dangling from a single strand of web attached to the lobe of my ear.

One time I thought I had solved the spider problem by dousing the walls with a hose having a high pressure nozzle attached to it.

But, that only made the spiders madder.

Like I went up to paint the trim and they rappeled over the gutter like some crack SWAT team and afffixed themselves to my face and shoulders.

I tried swatting them with a paint brush. Although that successfully removed the spiders, I had forgotten about the paint that was still on the brush. I looked like a jungle warrior who had his warpaint applied by someone on heavy duty drugs.

On one occasion, I put down one strip of paint and a spider came along and peeled it off as if it were a piece of birch bark.

At one point I rigged up a scaffold using a stepladder and a 55-gallon barrel. I figured I could dodge the feisty spiders easier on such a rig.

I was standing in the middle of the board, painting up a storm, when all of a sudden a big black spider slid down his web and landed directly on my nose.

CRACK

"Oh lordy!" I cried as the board broke in half and my body fell into a pool of paint on the ground.

A neighbor suggested I spray the house with a pesticide and then commence painting. Sounded logical.

I came back from the hardware store with a can of stuff guaranteed to kill any creepy crawler within 100-foot radius. With air gun in hand, I gassed the buggers.

After the smoke settled, I examined the wall. Not a spider to be found. Success at last.

I resumed painting. About a half an hour later, the world started spinning. Next thing I knew I was flat on my back recovering from the toxic fumes I had unwittingly inhaled.

The spiders, I learned, had hightailed it to the roof. They must have spent their time reproducing because when I returned there were three times as many of the hairy-legged creatures.

I found it most disturbing to accidentally paint over a spider and watch a spot of paint up and walk away. One wall had a polka dot pattern because of all the sleeping spiders I had inadvertently blanketed with latex.

And, there were all those spider tracks.

I have the only textured house in the neighborhood. Look closely and you'll see all these itty bitty spider prints meandering across the clapboard.

No way am I ever going to paint my house again. Let 'er peel, I don't care.

If anybody complains, I'll just rip the wood siding off and put up aluminum.

I can just hear the clamor of little spider bodies in the wind, hitting the siding like tiny clappers of a bell.

Love, death and a relentless snowblower

The following is rated TD, teenager discretion is advised. Adults should not read this without a teenager present.

With apologies to Stephen King, I offer the following tale..

People mistakenly believe that terror and the supernatural take a vacation when winter comes.

Beware. The macabre may come with the next snow..

On Dec. 18, 1972, Hotense Weems did a most dastardly thing. In love with another woman, Hortense did away with his wife and hid her body next to a snowblower in his garage.

The body of his wife was never found.

His crime was never discovered, and he later married his lover, a young sexy woman named Lucille. However, a short time later, Hortense died of a massive heart attack while shoveling snow... or so it seemed.

By order of his will, Lucille, inherited all his possessions, including a large snowblower tucked away in the garage.

In time the community forgot about the tragic affair of Hortense Weems, that is until the winter of '74.

Lucille had found another man and was once again a married woman. On January 10, 1974, a blizzard hit and covered the town with a foot of snow.

With her husband away, Lucille decided she would clear the walks with the snowblower Hortense had left her. Machinery held no mystery to her.

They say she was nearly finished with the driveway when a most bizarre and grisly accident occurred. Police suspect she must have tried to dislodge something caught in the snowblower blades when it pulled her into its whirling steel.

Through the years the snowblower passed among various owners until it became the possession of one Dudley Wimper, a teenager who had visions of making a lot of money clearing sidewalks in winter.

And, make money he did. Although unpopular at school, Dudley became legendary in his ability to remove snow.

People would remark that they had never seen man and machine work so well together as Dudley and his snowblower. No amount of snow could slow them down.

Dudley was devoted to his snowblower. After every job, he'd wipe it off and it seemed like he was forever lubricating it.

One day a strange thing happened. Dudley was clearing a walk when a bully from school began picking on him. The big guy picked up the frail-looking teenager and threw him into the snow. Then he began pelting Dudley with snowballs.

Mysteriously the snowblower slipped into gear and rolled toward the big kid standing over Dudley. He didn't notice the machine until it was too late.

Youthful reflexes saved the bully from certain death, they say. But, it didn't save him from losing his right leg to the machine.

One day while plowing a neighbor's driveway, Dudley met a girl and fell deeply in love. And, she grew to love him, too.

For a time Dudley gave up his snowblowing jobs. His snowblower sat rusting in his garage.

It was Dec. 18, 1982. Dudley and his girl were watching television when suddenly they heard an engine running. It sounded like it was right outside the kitchen door.

Suddenly the door burst open and there was the snowblower, its steel blades grinding the door into pulp. It devoured tables and chairs as it rolled through the kitchen into the living room.

Within moments it had the two teenagers trapped in a corner of the room and was moving slowly toward them.

The two teenagers were never seen again, nor was the snowblower ever found;

They say the blower roams the snow-covered streets of Northern Wisconsin towns, a killer machine fueled by the fury of a wife and a lover scorned.

So, the next time you walk home in the desolation of a winter's night and hear an engine in the distance, don't look back.

Retrieving ring no cinema romance

People mistakenly believe the only horror we experience is when we go to the movies.

They don't know about patio decks.

The other day I was out on the patio deck at the home of my wife's folks. I was half asleep in a chaise lounge sipping my second can of Old Milwaukee and reading the Kathleen Turner interview in *Playboy*.

Life doesn't get any better than that.

Anyway, there I was reading when my eldest daughter came up and for some reason known only to her, wanted me to come inside the house with her. "Daddy's busy," I told her gently.

Well, if you have small children, you know they rarely take no for an answer. Soon the kid was tugging at my hand. In the process, she managed to latch onto my wedding ring and to yank it right off my finger. The ring flew across the patio deck, bounced along the floor and disappeared between two boards.

"Oh, lordy!" I yelled as I jumped out of the chaise lounge. I ran over to where the ring had disappeared and peered through the spaces in the floor like a dog eyeing up a gopher hole.

My wife heard my hysterical scream and rushed out.

"What's going on here?" she asked.

"My ring, it's gone for good," I said pointing at the patio floor.

"No it isn't, silly... Just crawl under the deck with a flashlight."

"Are you crazy woman! You have any idea what lives under patio decks? Why, I've heard tales about rats as big as bulldogs and spiders so strong they can rip the cap off a Pepsi bottle!"

"Donald, have you been reading Stephen King again?"

"OK, OK, I'll do it, but on the condition you and the kids leave the house," I said nervously.

After the family had left, I went to the trunk of my car, pulled out a duffel bag full of camouflage combat gear. I slipped my .357 Smith and Wesson in the canvas web shoulder holster and put my carbon steel survival knife in its boot sheath.

I walked back to the deck, whipped out my Boy Scout flashlight and dropped to the ground. I dug my elbows into the moist soil and pulled my body under the deck.

The flashlight beam bounced off the back of a spider that, I swear, was as big as a pop bottle cap. "DIE CRAWLER" I screamed as I pulled the knife from my boot and swung it at the webslinger. Although I missed him, I at least scared the creature away.

Once again I pointed the flashlight ahead and lo and behold, there was the ring resting on a long forgotten orange peel. But, behind it was what appeared to be two yellow eyes.

"RAT!"

I pulled out the revolver and got off a quick shot. The bullet ricochetted off a rock, shot through the deck, crashed through the Thermopane patio door and, I later learned, shattered into dust a Waterford vase in my mother-in-law's china cabinet.

I later found out the eyes were two marbles my daughter had inadvertently tried to roll across the deck the day before.

I got my ring back, but that seemed unimportant to the police officer who was investigating reports of gunshots or the firefighters who were called to pull me out from underneath the deck.

Mitered corners, bare concrete don't last

I have finally figured out why I hate to shovel snow.

It's the same reason I don't make my bed in the morning.

I mean, why should I make a bed or shovel a walk when I know eventually both will get messed up anyway?

Take bedmaking, for instance.

How can anyone consider himself a rational being when he spends 10 to 15 minutes meticulously making a bed knowing full well that by day's end his own hands will rip those neatly tucked corners right off the mattress.

Heck, you mop a floor, you figure it's good for at least week.

That's why kids don't like making beds. They haven't learned this neurotic compulsion that comes with adulthood. Their virgin minds don't see any reason to do it. A bed is to sleep in, not look at!

And, their parents never offer any good reasons why they should make their beds.

"Johnny, make your bed this instant!" screams the harried mother.

"Why ma?"

"Because I said so!"

Or, parents will tell their kids that if they don't make their beds, their bedrooms will look messy.

Come on, who's going to see your bedroom? I don't know about you, but when I was growing up, the only people who saw the inside of my bedroom were my parents or good friends... and my friends could have cared less how my bedroom looked.

OK, if I was going to hold a formal dinner party in my bedroom, I'd make the bed.

Sometimes I'd compromise. I'd leave my covers in a mess, throw a bedspread over the whole works and smooth it down. It looked good as made to me.

The only time I made my bed voluntarily was when I was 15 or so and fate happened to deliver a *Playboy* magazine into my hands. Realizing the consequences of possessing such contraband, I hid the magazine under my mattress, and as an added precaution, I made my bed so my mother wouldn't go snooping around it.

Worked like a charm. She never nosed around the bed and the whole time she rejoiced because she thought her son had finally developed some character.

Anyway, snow shoveling is the same thing...

It's 5 p.m. You are really whipped. I mean, you're so tired you had to take a deep breath just to turn the ignition key of your car.

You drive home on streets so slippery you car slides around like butter on a hot griddle. Your nerves are so shot that if the guy behind you honked, you'd rip the turn signal lever right off the steering wheel column.

After arriving home, a sane and civilized person in that condition would head for the refrigerator, grab a beer and bury himself in the nearest easy chair.

But, what do we do?

We pull ourselves into the garage, grab a snow shovel and spend the next 45 minutes pushing snow.

There you are in the dark risking either cardiovascular gridlock or spinal dislocation. For what? A medal?

I'll tell you for what: A severe muscle spasm that will hit your legs and back in the middle of the night. Or, a head cold that will tie up your respiratory system for a week.

But, you did it. Your walk is pure concrete now. It's the cleanest walk in the whole neighborhood.

You hurt, but you're a hero.

So what happens?

The next morning you wake up, look out the window and discover your sidewalk and driveway are buried under another foot of snow.

What's worse is to wake up and discover the temperature rose 10 degrees overnight and the snow would have melted off the sidewalks anyway.

That's why, unless it's a darn blizzard, I wait at least a day before shoveling my driveway.

Heck, why should I do nature's work.

There are WHAT in my Garage!!!

Some people think the movie *Aliens* is scary. Hey, that's nothing compared to the gut retching, terror of...

Rrrring

"Hello?"

"Mr. Oakland, there are skunks living in your garage," said an anxious voice.

"Say what?"

"Three of them, I saw them go in..."

"Did you see them go out?" I interrupted.

"No."

"Oh. Well, what do you suggest I do?"

"Get rid of them, " the voice said somewhat impatiently.

"Uh, how would you suggest I go about doing that?"

"That's your problem," the caller said and hung up.

"Why me?" I said to myself as I looked out the window at the garage, its door half open. The one night I forget to close the door and a bunch of skunks think my garage is the Holiday Inn.

Like it's my fault they're in there. Like I should have been on the corner last night watching for the critters.

"Hey, you! Yeah, you skunks... whadaya think you're doing comin' into this neighborhood.... turn your butts south boys or meet Mr. 12 gauge here."

My thoughts snapped back to the present.

I just can't go in there and blow them away, I thought. Unlike alien monsters, skunks don't die graciously. They always leave a little something behind. If you've ever seen a dead skunk on the highway, you know what I'm talking about.

Can you imagine what would happen if one of those critters let loose in my garage? Why, the neighbors would string me up.

Years from now, a Realtor would pass down my street and tell his clients... "Yup, there used to be homes, families, a nice neighborhood here. Then one day this jerk went one-on-one with a skunk, and, well, they never could get rid of the odor. One by one the neighbors just moved out."

Someone suggested trapping the skunks.

Hey, I'd rather play soccer with a time bomb.

But, I had to do something. I mean, I could just see my eldest daughter running up to the garage and exclaiming: "Look daddy, a black and white kitty!" Kaboom.

The kid would never again be able to live a normal life.

Then a great idea, an inspired solution, hit me.

I rushed downstairs and ripped into a box containing things from my childhood. I grabbed a slingshot and a shiny ball bearing. I went up to the bathroom and covered the ball bearing with Vaseline. I decided against using a shotgun because it's such an obnoxious weapon and I have this tendency to blow out walls with them.

I went outside and approached the garage with caution. I slowly lifted the door and entered the dark and dusty building. It was so quiet in there, I could hear myself sweat. My eyes nervously scanned the clutter. Cobwebs brushed against my tightly drawn face and attached themselves to my perspiration soaked t-shirt.

My arms trembled as I drew back the slingshot. My plan was simple. Just as the skunk would turn to raise its tail, I would let loose with the slingshot, the ball bearing sort of corking his defense. Yeah, I'd have a pretty upset skunk on my hands, but I figured he'd get over it after he would leave for more suitable surroundings.

Slowly I walked, my slingshot moving side to side like Sonny Crockett's .45 on Miami Vice. My eyes studied every possible hiding place, searching for some movement, some hint of their presence. I knew I would have only a split second to fire.

Suddenly my eyes caught movement to my left. I turned and fired....

AAAAAAGH!

I kind of felt sorry for that big spider who at that moment chose to dangle in front of my eyes. He must have died instantly as that ball bearing from my slingshot slammed into him and hurled him across the room.

The ball bearing continued on, easily passing through the hull of my fiberglass canoe, glancing off a stud in the wall and crashing through three storm windows.

I retreated from the garage, my search-and-destroy mission for skuhks resulting only in the untimely death of an innocent spider.

I decided a less tactical and more strategic approach was called for.

By now word of the skunks in my garage had spread throughout the neighborhood. My phone was ringing constantly and neighbors were packing up their kids and driving off as if to run from some impending disaster. I guess few people shared my confidence in being able to bring this problem to a odorless ending.

I had to do something about those skunks. I couldn't shoot them. I couldn't trap them. I thought about gassing them out by letting my car run inside the garage, but someone told me it might kill them, but not before they would unleash their awesome spray.

Expert help was needed. So I got on the phone to Scott Craven, a University of Wisconsin-Extension wildlife expert in Madison. He was very reassuring.

No, they weren't taking up permanent residence in my garage. Most likely they only wanted to spend the night and then move on.

No, I didn't need to make like a Green Beret and go in after them with guns drawn.

He suggested that I just make life a little miserable for them. Then they'd leave on their own accord.

"How do you make a skunk miserable?" I asked.

"Hang moth balls in the garage," he said. "They hate the smell."

I thought that was a little weird because you wouldn't think a skunk would dislike any smell, considering the potent perfume they live with.

The second thing he suggested was to leave the lights on. Skunks hate lights.

That seemed reasonable enough. I can't sleep with the lights on either.

So I did both, but still I wasn't totally convinced it would do the job.

Then an idea hit me, a surefire way to get rid of the skunks. I rushed into the house.

It was such an obvious solution, I wondered how come nobody had ever thought of it before. Moments later, I walked out of the baby's room carrying a big garbage bag.

How better to fight a skunk than to beat him at his own game?

I slowly lifted up the garage door. When it was about half open, I carefully removed the wire holding the plastic bag closed.

"OK, skunks, take this!" I screamed as I unloaded a week's worth of dirty disposable diapers into the garage. The odor about flattened me.

About 10 seconds later, three skunks shot out from under the door. They nearly hit me as they tore down the driveway and disappeared down the block.

Some things are even more potent than skunk spray.

Living in fear of the fatal flush

I'm expecting Mt. St. Flush to erupt any day now.

I've been feeling the tremors.

If asked what is the most dangerous thing in a household, most people would probably answer the furnace, stove or garbage disposal.

Well, none of those things holds a candle to a dormant toilet.

I remember the last time our toilet became active. It was 6:30 a.m.; I was in the bathroom brushing my teeth.

Just before leaving the bathroom, I flushed the toilet. Except it didn't flush. The water disappeared from the bowl, but it didn't make any gurgling sound.

Suddenly the top of the toilet started rattling.

"Oh, lordly, she's going to blow!" I screamed as I turned to run out the door, except I had forgotten the door was closed.

"Honey, what's wrong?" My wife cried out from the bedroom after hearing the loud thud and subsequent groaning noises.

"Run for it dear, the toilet is about to erupt!"

By now the entire toilet was rocking violently.

"Do something, Donald," my wife exclaimed as she raced past the bathroom door.

"Like what?"

"Like shutting it off," she yelled from the living room.

"I don't know how to shut it off. Hey, if something doesn't have an on-off switch, I'm lost."

I picked myself off the floor.

"Where's the cat?" I asked.

"Why?"

"Well, I read once about how ancient tribes used to sacrifice virgins to appease an angry volcano. I figured the cat was the closest thing we had...

"You're sick," she snapped back

"Ah, heck, it's too late anyway, listen," I said in a hushed voice.

A dull thundering sound filled the room.

KABOOOM!

The explosion blew screens off every window the house.

My wife and I dashed out the front door as an awesome lava-like flow of sewage roared down the hallway, across the living room and cascaded out the doors.

It seemed like every toilet in the neighborhood was suddenly pouring its guts into our little procelain potty.

The gusher shot through the roof and went 30 feet high.

Heck, National Geographic wanted to photograph it for a cover story. The plume was really colorful when caught by the light of a mid-morning sun.

It took months to clean up from that last eruption. The only good that came of it was our grass seemed greener that year

Now we live in constant fear that such an event might happen again.

We have written all over the country for information on any seismographic device which we can install to forwarn us of an eruption.

We did see some research by a master plumber in Connecticut who suggests such eruptions can be predicted by an abrupt behaviorial change in household pets and a sudden, unexplained absence of spiders in one's basement.

I suspect the next eruption will come at the worst possible time. That's why I have been worried lately.

A week ago, I had a bit of intestinal distress, but that didn't bother me half as much as worrying that Old Mt. St. Flush might go on an awesome rampage again.

I stood there drinking down Kaopectate milkshakes and staring at the toilet for signs of impending doom.

Oh, I've taken preventive measures. There isn't a drain cleaner made that I haven't dumped into the porcelain belly of my toilet.

But, still I feel tremors.

It's really tough living with the fact the next flush might be your last.

Lawn upkeep is a pain in the grass

Every time I try to improve my lawn, Mother Nature humiliates me.

This year I decided to hang the expense and make a real effort to avoid having the worst front lawn in the neighborhood.

I mean, my lawn has been so bad in previous years, every time the wind picked up it was like Dust Bowl Days.

Instead of a soft blanket of grass in the backyard, I had rock-hard dirt. It was so hard, some neighbor kids wanted to make it into a basketball court.

"Enough is enough," I said to myself this spring. I packed up the VISA card and headed off to the store for some Grade A, Super-grow lawn fertilizer. Cost is no object, I vowed.

I kept repeating that phrase as the bill approached $40.

Figuring food is more important than how it is served, I bought a cheap spreader.

Wanting to surprise my neighbors with my soon-to-be lush lawn, I decided to spread this premium lawn food at night.

Big mistake.

I discovered how many shades of green grass you can produce when you miss spots with a cheap spreader.

But, I didn't care. At least the darn lawn was green and growing. For once I was able to use the lawnmower more than once a month.

Then I got really brave. I went out and bought a box of grass seed. I finally felt confident enough to fill in all those bare spots.

I was so proud when I saw those tiny blades of grass break through the soil. I even laid down and talked to them, encouraging them to grow. I promised I'd never let them go thirsty again.

True to my word I was.

Every other day, I faithfully watered the new grass.

I didn't let my kids get within 50 feet of it.

And, should a dog come anywhere near the house, I'd scream out of the house like a Chinese warrior and chase the mangy mutt down the block.

Nothing was going to deprive me of my green glory, except good ol' Mother Nature.

Just as my grass turned lush, Ma Nature turned dry. And, she stayed dry.

I watered and watered and wondered whether I'd have to sell my car to pay my water bill.

The watering didn't help, and ultimately I was forced to give up. My vegetable garden had a greater need for the water. I mean, it breaks your heart to see beet tops topple from thirst.

Consequently, green grass turned to yellow, soft blades turned stiff, ground turned to rock and little baby grasses just withered and died.

I could have bought three cases of beer and a bottle of good whiskey for what I wasted on that stupid lawn. There just isn't any justice in the world.

Late one night I found myself lying in my bone-dry back yard, alternately beating my fists against the powder-like dirt and shaking my arms toward the heavens.

"I have a dream, Mother Nature, and while you try your best to deny me it, I shall persist. Someday, maybe 10 years from now, you'll permit me a green lawn. Just once, so I'll have a story to tell my grandchildren before I die!" I cried.

What's needed here is a little lawn and order

'HOLD IT RIGHT THERE! PUT YOUR RAKE DOWN AND YOUR HANDS UP!"

A man wearing a green jumpsuit and holding a bullhorn appears from behind the garage.

"YOU'RE UNDER ARREST," He shouts through the bullhorn.

"For what?" I ask, rubbing my ears.

He puts down the bullhorn. "First degree grass abuse," he says, flashing a green badge in front of my face.

"You've been observed killing and maiming lawns," he continues.

"Hey, I love grass."

"We have evidence to the contrary," he says, as he makes a beckoning motion with one arm

A lady wearing camouflage fatigues and holding a Nikon camera with a 600mm night vision lens rises out of my pea patch.

"We have it all on film," he says with a sly smile.

"You've got to be kidding..."

"You have the right to remain silent, you have a right to an attorney or lawn and garden man.." he reads from a small card.

The two whisk me away to a nondescript building in downtown Wausau and throw me into a dimly lit room.

A large man wearing a gray three-piece suit walks in and sits down.

"I'm Garrison Green, grass attorney for Marathon County," he says as he brushes a few blades of grass off his sleeve.

"You're in big trouble, Mr. Oakland."

"I'm in trouble? Hey, last time I heard kidnapping was against the law. I've got my rights, you know!"

"Grass abusers have no civil rights, Mr. Oakland."

"What makes you so sure I'm a grass abuser, lawn boy."

"Mr. Oakland, we have documented numerous complaints from your neighbors who are greatly disturbed by your behavior on the lawn..."

"Hey, I've taken good care of my grass. Just the other day I spent $40 fertilizing it."

"You guys think you are so smart," the GA says shaking his head. "We saw you fertilizing, but we also saw you later that night taking handfuls of 27-3-3 and throwing it on poor unsuspecting sod. A couple of days later the grass yellowed. It is now near death... the victim of heinous overfertilization."

"Why would I do that?"

"Because you don't like grass. You guys are all alike. Love your mothers, hate your lawns. Did you like mowing lawns when you were a child?"

"I can't recall," I reply.

"You didn't. You hated it. You wanted to play baseball or fool around with the boys at the corner drugstore. But, no, you had to stay home mowing the grass. Now, you're getting even."

"Prove it!"

"Joyce!" In walks the woman who was hiding in my pea patch. She opens a large envelope and spills dozens of 8 x 10 photographs onto the table. Some show me knifing a section of grass with a spade. Others show me dumping handfuls of herbicide on my backyard.

"OK. OK, so I blew away a little grass, big deal!"

The GA smiles and gets up.

"Having confessed to your crimes, we sentence you to two years of hard yard work. Also, you are to attend grass school until you learn to control your urges.

"As part of your sentence, I hereby order you to accompany, Miss Mayberry, on her home and garden tours for senior citizens so that you will appreciate the beauty of residential greenery."

"No, no...NO!" I plead.

"Degenerate grass abusers must be mowed down wherever they appear. There must be lawn and order in our nation's neighborhoods." He turns to the woman. "What's our next case.

"A town of Rib Mountain man who refuses to pull dandelions."

How about some Lawn Aid, Willie?

We've got Farm Aid, Live Aid.. Gatoraid.

Well, I think it's time we have Lawn Aid.

Yes, sir, the time is ripe for a massive concert devoted to raising funds for my ailing lawn.

People don't realize lawnowners in Wausau are battling the fiercest drought since 1976.

Lawns are dying everywhere.

One or two thundershowers aren't enough. Unless we receive a two-day soaker, the fate of lawns in our fine community may be irreversible.

What is needed is massive amounts of water and fertilizer. And, as those of us who pay utility bills know, that requires money.

Green money for greener lawns!
Ah, come on, you say. Who can get excited about a lawn?
Heck, if we can throw an umpteen day bash for a statue in New York Harbor, we can surely have an afternoon of fun to benefit living lawns.
OK, so you don't care diddley about my lawn. I'm giving you an excuse to party, isn't that enough.
If you need something to appeal to your benevolent spirit so that you can in some perverse way justify your participation in this orgy for a cause, I submit to you a letter I wrote to Willie Nelson.

Dear Willie,
"Willie, you're a man of the soil and I think you can appreciate what is happening to lawns all over Wausau.
"They're dying of thirst, Willie.
"Willie, it makes you just want to cry when you get down on bended knee and watch closely as once healthy, green blades of grass turn yellow and whither. These little blades of grass who ask nothing more than to grow and get mowed, are dying by the thousands each day.
"Baby grasses, little itty-bitty blades of life are being burned to death by the summer's sun. Whole families of grass have been wiped out.
"And, you know what's happening, Willie? Weeds. Evil weeds are invading my lawn. Like carpetbaggers, they are taking advantage of the weakened Kentucky Bluegrasses and robbing them of life-sustaining water. Soon the grasses die and the weeds take over.
"Willie, unless this mindless onslaught is quelled, I will be forced to spray my lawn with every hebicide known to man. It's either that or face the wrath of neighbors who already are accusing me of having a lawn that is a breeding ground for noxious weeds. I'm not kidding. Some of them have compared me to Moammar Gadhafi harboring landscape terrorists bent on front yard anarchy.

"So, what I'm suggesting is you and the boys come over to my place and stage a concert. I'll charge $20 a ticket. You keep half, I'll keep 40 percent for administration. With the rest, you and me can head down to the K mart and get a bag or two of 26-10-10 or 10W40 or whatever. What change we get back, I'll put in a bank account to help pay future water bills.

"Now that you've done a number for the farmers, how about doing something for the rest of us?"
Sincerely,
Don Oakland

Hey, after reading that, if you don't feel choked up, you have no heart. Tell you what, if it'll make you feel better, we can all join hands, circle my house and pass out Grass Aid T-shirts. Maybe I could send you an 8 x 10 color photograph of dying grass to soften you up.

Give my lawn a new lease on life.

Evergreen is ever strong

Have you ever wanted to say something nice about someone, but never got around to doing it? Then one day you discover the person is gone or died and you really feel bad.

Tonight I feel that way about my Chinese evergreen.

I think it's dying.

I have taken drastic measures to reverse its decline, like giving it a new pot, some store-bought soil and a hefty dose of nutrient rich liquid fertilizer. But, still the plant looks pale.

For years it has survived phenomenal abuse and neglect. At times it has been down to only one leaf. But, just when I would think the plant was a goner, the darn thing would sprout a new leaf.

What strength! What cellular fortitude!

Oh, I know what you are saying.

"Hey, Mildred, you gotta read this! This guy's going nutso over a stupid plant. Can you imagine they actually pay people to write this stuff!"

OK, so most of you can't get all worked up over a lowly, nonflowering, green plant. Nevertheless, I feel compelled to tell you the story of my little plant. If you feel from this point on that your time would be better spent getting a beer, I understand.

About 10 years ago, I was browsing through the book department of a K mart store in LaCrosse when I came upon this small Chinese evergreen resting against several books. Obviously, someone had picked it up from the plant department and on his or her way out of the store, decided to abandon it in favor of some slushy novel.

I was touched. My heart went out for this orphaned plant and I impulsively bought it. Heck, it was only $1.50.

At the time it was the only plant I owned. I didn't know the first thing about caring for plants other than to periodically water them.

For some reason which now escapes me, I became hooked on plants. I filled my apartment with them. Aloe, coleus, and sit down for this, a banana tree. No fooling, a 4-foot tall banana tree grew next to my easy chair. It was in a pot the size of a bushel basket and weighed a ton. The tree got so big I started worrying about squirrels.

My little Chinese evergreen thrived in the jungle that was my living room.

Then I started dating a girl and later got married, and all of a sudden plants were no longer important to me. One by one I got rid of them. In the end only two remained: The aloe, because I heard it was good for burns, and the Chinese evergreen.

In recent years I admit I have neglected the lowly little Chinese plant. When you have two children around the house, you tend to forget about horticultural obligations. What made matters worse, I don't think the plant ever fully recovered from a run-in it had with my wife's cat several years back.

Despite infrequent waterings and the ignominy of having to live in an environment of dirty diapers and a screaming infant, the plant struggled on.

It just won't give up. Maybe it's the plant's oriental heritage, a Zen-like obligation to survive against all odds.

Yanked from the ground at birth, taken from the company of its fellow plants, orphaned in its youth and left for dead on a K mart shelf, and now so abused in its maturing years. I tell you, a plant deserves better.

I must add a postscript to the above essay written about a year and a half ago. I moved the Chinese evergreen from the baby's room to the kitchen. I placed it next to a half dozen other flowering plants on top of the microwave.

For many, many months the plant seemed to be in a state of suspended animation. It was a plant with one leaf that refused to give up. Then one day to my utter amazement out sprouted a new leaf.

At this writing I expect the leaf to unfurl within a matter of weeks. I tell you, this is one tough plant. Now wasn't this an inspiring story?

Pentagon Peas are costly to grow

I've got Pentagon peas in my garden.

A new variety of legume? Not quite.

They are products of the federal government style of horticulture, which is the belief that the more one spends on one's garden, the better it will be.

As a consequence, I have peas that cost me dollars to grow instead of fractions of a cent. Heck, if the Pentagon can spend $3,000 for a wrench, I can invest a $1.50 in a pea plant.

When a federal plan gardener is asked why he spends so much money, he'll invariably answer: "To save money."

"Just think of all the money we will save not having to buy vegetables," I explain to my wife.

"And, when you can all those veggies, we'll be able to extend our savings well into winter," I continue.

"What do you mean, when I can?" she snaps back.

"Well, it is an unwritten law that he who grows and harvests, shall not can. I mean, how many farmers do you know who have their own canning plants?"

"OK, I guess I can do it. Considering your past success at vegetable gardening, it shouldn't take but a few minutes," my wife said with a quiet little laugh.

People don't realize how hard gardening is nowadays.

Don't believe what you see on the TV. Especially those shows which say you can grow enough to feed a family of five on only a few cents a season. Those World War II Victory Gardens were just a cruel hoax created by seed companies.

First thing a gardener needs is a book. You can't grow anything without a book. Hey, gardening is a science. Gone are the days when you just plopped seeds into the ground.

I don't know why it is, but gardening books seem to be twice as expensive as ordinary books.

You can't buy a decent gardening book for under $15 anymore.

And, one will never do. Just when you are about to grow that Victory Garden, you'll decide to try the square foot gardening method instead. That requires you to buy another book.

And, maybe next season you'll experiment with wide-row planting and you'll need to buy yet another book.

Heck, my gardening library now resembles a set of encyclopedias.

If you don't have much room for a garden, then you must intensify your gardening efforts.

That means building box gardens and cold frames at $20 to $50 a shot. And, you'll have to build an elaborate trellis system for your vertical crops.

You'll have to buy a fence, else nasty rabbits will eat everything you plant or your kids will vandalize your veggies after mistaking your box garden for a sand box.

You'll kiss $75 or more goodbye accomplishing all that.

But you're not through spending money just yet.

You've got fertilize the darn thing. And, it seems every vegetable requires a different type. Your spinach needs 10-10-10 while your beets have got to have 5-10-15.

What I end up doing is buying a half dozen types of fertilizer and mixing them. Hey, why not let the plants decide which type they want?

Of course, no self-respecting city gardener would be without compost. Although the stuff you put into your pile is free, you've got to buy something called compost starter. That shoots the better part of $10.

Because I don't have a cow, I have to buy manure at the store in bags costing $1 to $2 a piece.

I refuse to ask a farmer for manure. I don't have a truck to haul it in and my wife nearly killed me when I once hauled it home in the back seat of her car.

Tools-- you'll need lots of them for your garden. Heck, I'll walk into a hardware store for a package of seed and walk out of there with $30 in new tools.

And, you're still not done buying. You still have to buy dozens of peat pots and bags of potting soil for your transplants.

After all that, if you have any money left, you might buy one last item: Seed.

Black bottom is tomato dance of death

This is a tragic tale of tomatoes.

My tomatoes died a terrible death. Their bottoms went black.

Not just one, but every blasted one of them succumbed to this ugly disorder.

My gardening books say the poor things had something called blossom end rot. And, what an insidious plant killer it is. I mean, you see a bountiful harvest of tomatoes on the vine and just after they turn red, their undersides turn black.

The books told me it's caused by a lack of calcium in the soil.

Well, excuse me! Maybe I should have watered them with milk

"A gallon a day keeps the blossom rot away," I would have sung as I doused them with a jug of 2 percent.

The books say that although the bottom of the tomato looks like the black plague hit it, the remaining portion of the tomato is still good and can be eaten.

Not by this seedslinger, by golly. I don't eat ugly vegetables.

Anyway, I couldn't stand to watch those tomatoes suffer, so the other day I pulled up the whole works.

In minutes a record crop was wiped out.

I was heartsick and frustrated as I threw each plant onto the concrete driveway. I felt like taking one of those bright green tomatoes and throwing it at the garage door, but I decided against it for fear of teaching my daughters bad habits.

My eldest daughter had already learned what fun it is to pick tomatoes off the vine and watch them roll down the driveway.

This wasn't the first tragedy to befall the Oakland garden this fateful year.

Maggots got my radishes. What a gruesome death they suffered. They were such beautiful young plants, the best radishes I had ever grown.

Then one day in late spring, I pulled one of the large plants from the soil, wiped it off and took a bite. Delicious!

I had about finished it when I looked down and saw looking up at me this little white worm.

I dropped the radish and clutched my throat. I was totally, nearly mortally, grossed out.

After I had sufficiently recovered, I pulled up another radish and split it open with a jackknife. Four little worms poked their heads out.

I pulled out my red bandana, wiped a tear from my eye, and then spaded under the whole crop. All that work growing these vegetables and all I have to show for it is a bunch of fat maggot larvae.

You feel so guilty after you have destroyed a crop. Was it something I did? Did I water too much or too little?

Maybe if I would have spent that extra day weeding, things might have turned out differently.

Maybe if I would have bought the expensive fertilizer instead of that generic stuff those plants would have made it.

It's all very agonizing. In fact, that's where I think the word agriculture comes from... a bunch of people (a culture) in agony.

Even the weather did a number on me this year.

First, it was darn dry.

Then came a windstorm which blew down my pole beans just before the harvest. Having raised those babies from seed, I was shattered.

I picked up the tangled mass of green vines, stared into the sky and screamed: "AAAAAAAARGH!!!"

Oh, there were successes. Had an outstanding pea crop.

My Swiss Chard is growing like a weed, which really burns my wife because she hates the stuff.

I would have had a dandy spinach crop this year, but my eldest daughter decided to turn one of my raised gardens into her personal sand box. She had pulled up a dozen plants before I had realized what she was up to.

I tell you, it's a hard life we men of the soil lead.

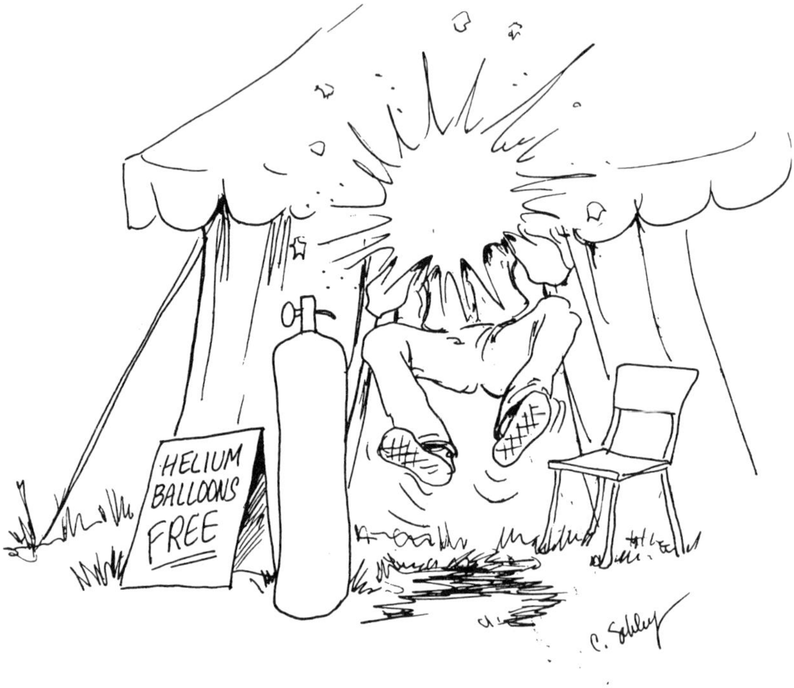
HELIUM
BALLOONS
FREE

Chapter Seven

Fair tent duty bursts reporter's bubble

There are times when your boss will ask you to do something which is not exactly within your job description. Sometimes such extra duty can turn into quite an adventure. It happened to me one day while working for the Daily Herald...

When they asked me if I would work a shift in the Daily Herald's tent at the Wisconsin Valley Fair, I jumped at the chance.

Although I have visited many county fairs, I never have had the opportunity to work one. It was exciting just thinking about hawking papers like a pitchman along the midway.

"Step right up and take a shot at the best-read newspaper in town. Only 25 cents or three for a dollar. Buy a subscription and win your girl a Kewpie doll."

Unfortunately, that's not how the assignment turned out.

Friday morning I eagerly reported for work.

The tent commander informed me that it would be my duty to sell newspapers, solicit donations to the Statue of Liberty campaign and answer any and all questions about our local paper.

"Right chief!" I said as I did my best Boy Scout salute.

"However, most of the time you will be blowing up balloons and giving them out to kids," he said, pointing to a tank of helium.

I panicked.

"But, sir, I've never blown up balloons before."

The tent commander just smiled. "By the end of the day, you will have learned."

Through all my years of extensive schooling, never once did I learn how to tie off an inflated balloon. Oh, there were times I blew up balloons with my own breath, but I always found someone to tie them for me.

"Don't worry, son, you'll get the hang of it. Uh, I got to get back to the office," he told me. With that the tent commander disappeared into the crowd.

The helium tank started hissing at me. I hissed back and grabbed another balloon. I carefully slipped it over the nozzle and began inflating it.

Suddenly the balloon shot off the nozzle like a ground-to-air missile and struck a rather well-endowed woman right below the neck. Somewhere out there is a woman who thinks the Daily Herald employs perverts.

I put on another balloon and held it with a death grip. Unfortunately, I forgot to turn off the valve.

KABOOM!

I dropped to my knees and grabbed at my heart. A dozen people gathered around and wondered if I had just shot myself. I thanked them for their concern as I picked a piece of balloon off my glasses.

Later on I found myself struggling with a knot when a small boy came up to me.

"Can I have a balloon, mister?"

"Just a minute, kid."

He soon was joined by two other tykes.

"Can we have a balloon, please?" they said in unison.

"Uh, why don't you guys come back later."

"We want one now," one youngster replied.

The balloon was beginning to cut off the circulation to my thumb.

"Bug off, kid!" I yelled.

"Boy, what a nerd, he can't even tie a balloon," the kid snapped back.

I whipped around. "Here kid! You want a balloon, go fetch it." I let go of the blue balloon and it flew high into the air and disappeared behind a food stand.

I blew up another balloon and put it in my mouth. My plan was to hold it there while I tied it off with a string. But, for some unknown reason my jaw loosened, causing me to swallow a balloon full of helium.

About a half dozen kids suddenly broke into laughter. I turned around and yelled, "Get outta here, you little." Well, the effect of the helium on my vocal cords made me sound like an over-ripe gremlin. Horrified, the kids took off down the midway.

Afraid to speak or blow up any more balloons, I had to take drastic action. I grabbed a pen and paper and made up a big sign:

"Sorry, no balloons. Out of helium."

I placed the sign outside the tent and hid behind a newspaper for the rest of the day. In my opinion, that's the only way to work a fair booth.

Modern technology may bury us all

In the world of work, often we are confronted with unusual challenges brought about by changing technology. Here's a report on one such challenge.

One day the maintenance department at the Daily Herald installed a new towel dispenser in the men's room.

You might think that's pretty insignificant, but I feel such things are worth noting.

I assume the management of the Herald, being enlightened to the feminist cause, installed a similar machine in the women's restroom; however, discretion prohibited me from verifying this in person. I considered standing outside the door and asking those who passed by on the accommodations within, but I discarded the idea because it might gain me a rather bizarre reputation.

Ever since I have been at the Herald, the men's room has had a crank type towel dispenser. When functioning, it did an adequate job. It was nice because if you had the muscle endurance in your right arm, you could crank out miles of toweling, a useful feature should you decided to bathe in the washbasin.

However, the new machine doesn't have a crank, which undoubtedly will save considerable amount of employee energy, thereby increasing productivity.

With this new machine all one has to do is pull down on the towel and it will automatically advance and cut off a predetermined length. With a ca-chunk sound, the machine then positions another towel for grabbing.

It is a truly an awesome marvel of modern technology.

However, there is one thing that has me stumped. On the right hand side is a little two word message: "Emergency Feed."

I have searched in vain for anything which explains what constitutes emergency feed. What emergency would require a paper towel?

I went back to my desk, set aside my work and began to ponder this perplexing question. I resolved I would do no more work until I found a solution to the paper towel puzzle.

Perhaps it is for a particularly distraught person with dirty hands who uses so much soap and water, a single paper towel wouldn't suffice.

Rather than go back to his desk sopping wet, he would press emergency feed and dry himself with yards of toweling.

Perhaps emergency feed is a safety feature to be used when the toilet won't flush.

I can imagine flushing the john and instead of the water going down it starts rising like some Hawaiian volcano.

In this situation, toilet paper would be woefully inadequate. So, I could see the flushee racing to the paper towel dispenser, hitting emergency feed and filling the bathroom with toweling, thereby drying up the floor before anybody discovers the mess.

What if someone in the newsroom suddenly decided to have a baby right on the city editor's desk?

As we all know, when a baby is on its way into the world it requires hot water and clean towels. I could see some resourceful reporter bursting into the men's room, hitting emergency feed on the towel dispenser and returning with sufficient toweling to swaddle the little babe.

Whatever it is, I don't think emergency feed should only be limited to towel dispensers. I think they should be standard equipment on toilet paper dispensers, particularly those which dispense about an inch and a half of tissue per pull. I'm talking about those dispensers with the lock on the top.

Although I won't go into gory details as to why I think this would be a practical feature, suffice it to say, it would be, uh, comforting to have.

I think the Herald should sponsor an interdepartmental seminar on the proper use of the emergency feed button on towel dispensers. Maybe only certain people in the office should be given the authority to operate the emergency feed feature. Emotionally, it might be too much for some of us to handle.

Like I worry about the day the dispenser decides to shift into emergency feed on its own. I can see myself washing up after a dirty day in the newsroom and becoming buried under a ton of toweling.

The gang gets goofy at doughnut time

I believe anybody who works in an office can relate to this eyewitness report written a couple of years ago...

When someone brings doughnuts into the Herald's newsroom, things get strange.

Maybe it's because it's such a rare occurrence that anyone here springs for sweets.

Of course, no one is ever encouraged to treat anymore.

I mean, if you bring in a bag of doughnuts and Danish, it's as if you're the house cat that just deposited a dead mouse on the kitchen floor.

Everybody suddenly is on a diet. It's as if the entire newsroom staff is massively obese and one more calorie will bust their bulges.

But, for all the moaning and lamenting, few ever turn down a treat.

The very mention that someone is buying doughnuts starts the staff acting very peculiarly.

"Hey, gang, (name deleted to protect the guilty) is going for doughnuts," someone announces in the newsroom.

For a moment there is absolute silence. All work stops. It's like one of those E.F. Hutton commercials.

Although everybody resumes working, subtle changes in behavior begin to surface.

Editors become increasingly nervous, tapping their fingers on the desk as they read stories.

They make quick glances around the room and then stare longingly at the door through which the doughnut carrier will enter.

Fifteen minutes pass.

Some reporters are pacing in front of their desks. Others sit silently in front of their video display terminals staring at blank screens, their fingers nervously drumming next to the keyboard.

Half an hour passes.

There is noticeable tension in the newsroom. Nobody talks, they just give each other quick glances, then turn their attention to the door.

"She's back," someone yells.

Suddenly everybody jumps up. They lean toward the door as the doughnut courier appears. As she walks through the newsroom, all eyes focus on the box in her hands. She sets it down in the middle of the room and opens it.

An editor leaps over his desk and lands next to the table where the doughnuts sit. A reporter lunges forward.

The editor growls, his back arches up and forward. His eyes burn into the eyes of the young reporter. The reporter growls back as their heads draw close above the open box.

Others in the room fidget and circle around the two. No one speaks, but some utter low grunts and whines.

The editor snarls loudly and the reporter backs off. The editor slowly turns and glares at the other staff members around him, then looks down into the box.

With lightning speed his hand scoops up a jelly roll out of the box and into his mouth. He quickly retreats behind his desk as he wipes the sugar from his chin.

The circle of staff cautiously closes around the box. Reporters eye each other suspiciously.

A hand reaches into the box for a glazed doughnut, but another faster hand reaches it first and whisks it away. A reporter's cry of agony echoes through the room.

Two women reporters grapple for a long john, finally ripping it in half before withdrawing to their desks.

A reporter from sports grabs two chocolate doughnuts and with an alley-oop hook sends one flying to his compatriot across the room.

Within minutes the box is empty. Editors are once again editing; reporters are once again writing. Every so often a groan of ecstasy is heard as someone bites into a jelly-filled pastry.

A certain columnist, afraid of the vicious pastry-feeding frenzy, sneaks up to the box for his feast of crumbs.

Uncluttered desk is unnatural

Sometimes we do things without realizing the full implications of our actions.

Take for instance what happened at work the other day. It all started when the person whose desk is next to mine decided it was time to clean the clutter of paper off her desktop.

I don't know what possessed her to do it. When I discovered what she was up to, I tried strenuously to dissuade her.

There are certain things in an office you don't tamper with: The boss's secretary, any wall socket having more than three holes, the coffee machine and a cluttered desk.

There is an ugly myth in American business that a cluttered desk is a sign of inefficiency and sloth.

The truth is an uncluttered environment is unnatural. If you doubt that, just look around come fall. Does Mother Nature pile her leaves neatly? No way.

The best working environnment for maximum productivity is one which more closely resembles nature.

But, that's not the point here.

Clutter doesn't occur overnight. It builds gradually, almost imperceptibly. As it grows, it interacts with other clutter.

Clutter, you see, seeks out clutter.

Over a period of weeks, a very delicate community of clutter is created. Each pile of paper is interdependent upon some other pile.

This is not unique to offices. Everything around us is clutter. Why, we are nothing more than a hodge-podge of cluttered cells held together with skin and bones.

This relationship between stacks of papers, piles of memos and bulging file drawers is so subtle we don't realize it exists. We just think the office is messy.

That's the trouble with most of us, we only look at the surface of things.

OK, one day someone decides to clean his or her desk. Here's what happens:

All of a sudden, the chain is broken, the community is disrupted and the stability of the entire office is threatened.

We don't notice it at first, but stacks of paper begin shifting.

A piece of paper we toss on a pile mysteriously slips off onto the floor.

Like a nuclear reaction, this phenomena builds inexorably.

I tell you, I'm fearing for my life because the gal next door cleaned her desk. You see, there is this huge stack of papers and books on top of a file cabinet separating our two desks.

At any moment this mountainous stack could come crashing down on me because of her insensitivity to the scheme of things. I can just see the headlines: "Reporter killed when struck by Webster's Third World Dictionary and two copies of the Wausau City Budget...workers find him buried under two feet of old news releases."

Although it was never reported in the popular press, there was this business reporter at a Boise, Idaho, newspaper who caused great damage one day by cleaning off two years worth of clutter from her desktop. Her misguided neatness caused a chain reaction which buried alive two copy editors. So fierce was the paper avalanche, it psychologically scarred for life a city editor and school board reporter.

It's best to leave clutter well enough alone.

You can be organized and messy, too.

Just like the beaver, one of the most efficient creatures in the world, you can surround yourself with a massive heap of stuff and still get the job done.

If you have to be neat, then have your office manager put your desk in the basement where you can't hurt anyone but yourself.

And, the next time someone criticizes you for having a messy desk, just tell yourself that it is truly unfortunate that such unenlightened people still exist.

Little do they know, it is you who keeps the office from the brink of disaster.

VDT games get bleeped

During my career in newspapering, I progressed from a manual typewriter with worn ribbon to sophisticated computer terminals which crashed without warning. Once I suggested our newsroom computers needed a different kind of software upgrade...

You know what I want for Christmas? A couple of computer games like Space Invaders.

But, I want them for use at the office, not at home.

Let me back up a bit.

Reporters at the Daily Herald type stories on computer terminals called VDTs, video display terminals. If you can imagine slamming a portable television set onto the top of an electric typewriter, you've got some idea what VDTs look like.

They're sort of a professional version of the home computers you see advertised on television.

Well, I've been after Dave Downing, the Herald's electronics technician, to do some creative modifications on my terminal.

At first I figured he could jiggle the circuitry around so I could pick up television signals. I mean, this thing does have a picture tube in it.

I figured all one would have to do would be to put up an antenna, run a few wires into the terminal, add a tuning circuit and then sit back and watch Channel 9.

It would be so nice. In between writing stories I could watch "General Hospital."

Downing seemed unenthused.

"Well, how about cable then? You could just plug it in a hole in the back."

"Think of it man! You could superimpose the typing function over the cable function so I could write my stories and watch HBO at the same time."

He started to walk away.

"I've seen televisions with smaller tubes than the one in my VDT, so it can be done."

He didn't turn around. But, as he left I heard him muttering about the VDT tube having more lines than a television tube and therefore being incompatible with a television signal.

"I bet if you were Japanese you could do it!" I yelled at him.

He walked faster and looked around to see if anybody was watching.

"Look, Edison never would have invented the telephone had he worried about compatibility."

That stopped Downing dead. He swung around on one foot.

"Edison invented the light bulb, Bell invented the telephone and a thousand and one Japanese couldn't turn your terminal into a television. So forget it."

Forget it? Hardly! I know when I've got a good idea, I thought to myself.

Heck, you get the idea and the rest comes easy in the inventing game, I continued muttering to myself.

It wasn't a minute later that inspiration hit again. I called him back to my desk.

"Why not alter the circuitry a bit to accept computer games?" I suggested.

"I could put a game box under my desk, run a few wires up through the bottom of the terminal and begin playing," I continued.

He shook his head and laughed. But, this time I sensed that his rejection was not on technical grounds. Rather, he felt the management of the Daily Herald wouldn't appreciate such tampering.

"Hey, I wouldn't tell anyone," I said.

He walked away. I was shot down again.

However, for the next several minutes I thought about the possibilities...

I'm at my terminal busily writing some routine piece of daily journalism. It's a boring story and I need a break.

I glance around to see if anybody is watching. I hit a secret switch underneath the desk. Instantly the story disappears and Space Invaders replaces it.

I begin pounding the keys at breakneck speed as little dots zip across the green screen and while others explode into brilliant flashes. There is no sound. Those circuits have been eliminated for obvious reasons.

Meanwhile, over at the city desk the editors take notice of the rapid typing sounds coming from my corner of the room.

"You know, in the past couple of weeks, Oakland has sure been writing a lot. He's always busy at his terminal," one editor says.

"But, it's odd. I haven't noticed any increase in the number of stories I have read with his name at the top," the other editor says.

"Well, his work habits are certainly an inspiration to all his co-workers," the first editor continues.

Meanwhile, I'm pushing my score up into the six figures.

Some Japanese customs don't belong here

I'm worried that businessmen might become samurai warriors in three-piece suits.

You see, there was this ad in the Wall Street Journal for a new book called "Fighting to Win: Samurai Techniques for Your Work and Life."

The ad says: "Before you confront a corporate adversary (or an angry spouse), consult an ancient ally: The samurai warrior."

I haven't seen or read the book, but nevertheless I'm worried.

Can you imagine what doing business would be like if everyone took this author's advice?

Wausau Insurance Companies would cease to exist. Rather, it would become "The Dynasty" with a shogun instead of a chief executive officer.

Promotions would be handled differently...

A young executive bursts through the door of the Claims Department.

"I wish to see the warlord!" he demands.

The secretary notices a certain icy gleam in his eyes. She has seen it many times before. "Mr. Jones is here to see you. I think he wants to talk about his advancement in the department."

The young lady then dives under her desk.

Moments later the Claims Department vice president walks into the room. "What can I do for you Jones?" he says sternly.

The young man takes a step back, unbuttons his suit coat to expose a long-handled sword.

"So, Mr. Jones, you think you are ready to become an executive," the vice president says. "Let us see how well you have learned the ways of the corporate samurai!"

He reaches into a drawer in the secretary's desk and pulls out a four foot long sword.

"HEEEE YAH!" he yells as he assumes a combat stance.

The young man quickly draws his sword and in a smooth motion sweeps it across the secretary's desk, slicing the telephone in half.

"BONSAI!" The elder vice president leaps over the desk and with a mighty thrust of his sword knocks the young man into the door. The young man recovers and attacks.

The power of his youth drives the vice president back against the wall. The young man positions himself for the fatal thrust when suddenly the secretary rams a wooden stick into his shin.

The vice president jumps away from the wall, turns and with a Reggie Jackson-like swing scares off the young man.

"Thank you, Miss Smith," he says to his secretary as he helps her to her feet. "You can't type worth a darn, but by golly, can you handle a staff."

And, should the company shogun find one of his department vice presidents (also known as feudal warlords) not producing, he wouldn't fire him. Samurai don't fire people...

Harry, vice president of finance, works late one night in his top floor office. Suddenly and very unexpectedly, the company shogun walks through the door.

"Yes lord," Harry says respectfully.

"Corporate profits have dipped 43 percent in the last quarter. We have yet to show any earnings increase in the past three quarters. I am displeased."

"But, lord, ever since American corporate executives adopted the ways of the samurai, our workers comp claims have gone out of sight. Do you have any idea how much it costs to stitch up a sword wound?"

The shogun scowls.

"I am displeased," he says as he walks out the door.

"Old grouch," the vice president says under his breath. He returns to his investments report unaware of the black-suited figures silently crawling through the window behind him.

The two ninja hidden by black hoods creep up behind him. One of them pulls out a dagger. Instinctively the old vice president turns and ducks as the knife falls past his head.

He jumps out of his chair, hits one of the assailants with a cigarette lighter and gives a karate kick to the other. He races out the door to safety.

Who knows, such samurai philosophies might even reach into the ranks of newspaper reporters and columnists.

Why, after reading this particular report, the publisher might hand yours truly the ceremonial sword of hari-kari and point toward the restroom door.

Raiders of the Abandoned Desk

When someone leaves the office for another job, the desk raiders appear.

They come in the night to plunder the treasures left hidden in the drawers of a freshly vacated desk.

Within minutes, what was once their co-worker's is now theirs.

No office is safe from them, not even the newsroom of the Daily Herald.

A while back a reporter left for a newspaper job out west. The minute she was out the door, desk raiders were going through her drawers.

That's stealing! You say.

A desk raider is no thief. He merely reallocates office resources.

The things a person leaves behind belong to the company. So long as those things never leave the office, you can't consider them stolen.

Anyway, desk raiding is the fastest way office workers can upgrade their desk supplies.

You see, veteran office workers are discriminated against when it comes to asking for office supplies.

Say you need a new stapler. Well, if you'd go up to the officer manager and ask for a new one, why he'd look at you as if you had just suggested selling his mother into slavery.

"Why do you need a new stapler?" he'd ask. Before you could respond he'd recite a long list of reasons why you really don't need one.

"My gosh, there must be ten good staplers in your department, just borrow one... You've gotten by all these years with the one you have... Maybe your stapler can be fixed... Our budget is really tight right now, ask me again a couple of months from now...use paperclips instead..."

Now, if a new employee finds his desk without a stapler and asks for a new one, he'll get one-- no questions asked. You see, the office manager doesn't want the new employee to think he has joined a chintzy outfit.

Everybody benefits from a desk raider's derring-do.

The desk raider gets a no-hassle replacement of defective equipment.

The new employee feels that the company really cares about him.

And, the office manager thinks he's made one of his employees happy without giving him a raise.

There is a lot of skill involved in good desk raiding.

Preparation is critical.

As soon as the desk raider hears someone is leaving, he's at his or her desk.

"Gee, I hear you're leaving. Gosh, that's too bad," he says with a hint of sadness.

Then nonchalantly he asks, "By the way, when is your last day?" The answer establishes the date of the raid.

The raider closes in: "Can I borrow a pencil?" It's a ploy so that he can reconnoiter the inside of the drawer.

Like a treasure hunter guarding a sunken Spanish galleon, the desk raider will hover around the desk on the employees's last day.

When everyone leaves for the day, the raider strikes.

In moments he has the stapler. The wastepaper basket is exhanged with his own. He checks out the chair. If it's better, it's gone.

Paperclips, rubber bands, pencils with erasers (prized because they are so rare) and file cards disappear into the raider's quick grasp.

To the desk raider a full roll of Scotch tape is like gold.

Some desk raiders have even been known to switch phones. There are legends told about desk raiders who have switched entire file cabinets and desks.

The real pros can go through a desk, take what they need, but leave just enough so the desk appears as it did when the co-worker left. It's a real art.

No dishonor at the honor box

Whoever invented the honor box should be drawn and quartered by turbo-charged Toyotas.

What is insidious about these honor boxes is the way they encourage the consumption of all the things you shouldn't be consuming.

A while ago I worked in an office which had one of these honor boxes filled with candy, snacks, and a wide assortment of belly-busting junk foods. The box was just kitty-corner from my desk.

Every time I sat down, I had to look at those packages of potato chips, Oreo cookies and Three Musketeers.

Even though I was not hungry at the time, I would suddenly feel hungry. I would feel like eating a candy bar, just one to tide me over until lunch or quitting time.

I figured that after six months of working with this convenient candy counter, I'd have to buy a whole new wardrobe. Heck, my belt had already become an abdominal tourniquet.

These honor boxes are worse than vending machines. I mean, with a vending machine you only have only one of a particular item displayed. With honor boxes, all the evils are in glorious view.

With a vending machine you have to plug it with a pocket full of change if you want more than one item.

With honor boxes you can stuff a couple of dollar bills into the slot and walk off with an armful of nutritional mayhem.

Why, one day I walked off with a package of Lorna Doones, some Sour Cream and Onion potato chips, a pack of peanuts and a Baby Ruth bar. It wasn't until 10 minutes later, after I had consumed the whole works, that I realized what nutritional upheaval I had wrought on my system.

The other evil of these honor boxes is they make you feel good every time you buy something.

After you put your money in the box, you subconsciously pat yourself on the back for being so honest.

You could have just taken the candy and not paid. But you didn't. You earned yourself yet another merit badge on your way to heaven.

While you are feeling so proud of yourself, you forget about how all that junk you are about to eat is going to put you on the fast track to premature death.

Honor boxes make it so easy to become a junk food junkie.

At least vending machines occasionally don't work. Every so often they take your money and keep your sweets.

Honor boxes always deliver.

And, they are never, ever empty. Sometime in the middle of the night an angel of obesity descends upon the office and refills the box with fresh delights.

The next morning these bars, chips and cookies sing like sirens, luring me ever closer to the complete collapse of my waistline.

The only way I can fight off their charms is to go across the street to the bakery to buy a sweet roll.

Software, hardware-- a profile of professions

It seems to me a business to get into is fixing computers. Seems like computers are forever crashing or getting bytes screwed up.

One day at the Daily Herald, they hired two types of computer specialists to sort out a problem. One specialist, called a hardware man, worked on the computer itself. The other, called a software man, worked on the programming.

I got to thinking about these two jobs as I worked on a story. I was typing the story on a typewriter rather than my computer because these two specialists had managed to crash the Herald's computer system.

If I had my choice, I'd be a hardware man.

He's a real macho mainframe kind of guy.

A software man is the type who likes to have flowers on his desk.

A hardware man drives up in a heavy-duty, turbocharged, black four by four with an "I Eat Apples for Lunch" sticker on the back bumper.

The software man pulls up in an old yellow Volkswagen Beetle and sits there listening to "Best of Boy George" tapes.

A hardware guy talks tough when he talks at all. He has the looks of Tom Selleck and the disposition of Clint Eastwood.

"Our computer isn't working," says the kindly newspaper publisher.

"You want it fixed, cough up $100 an hour plus expenses," the hardware man says as he eyes the secretaries in the front office.

"Sure, anything you want. Are you sure you can fix it?" the publisher asks as he backs away.

The hardware man's eyes narrow and he gives the publisher a long, angry look. "Boy, there isn't a computer built that I can't knock the chips out of. Where is it?"

The publisher points to the computer room and then quickly retreats into his office. The hardware man slings his bag of tools over his shoulder, spits the cigar from his mouth and walks toward the newsroom.

"I'm taking her down," he announces in a loud, authoritative voice.

"Oh, but you can't," cry out several editors. "We're on deadline."

"Tough! When I say she's going down, she goes down--like now," he growls.

"But, sir," one of the editors protests.

"Look, word wimp, you squawk once more time and I'll put so many bugs into your computer that when you cough the thing will crash." Minutes later the system goes down as the newsroom silently weeps.

Then there is the Southern California species of software man.

"Can you help us? Our computer is giving us all sorts of troubles," says the worried publisher.

"I can relate to that," he replies in a soft, reassuring voice.

"I gotta have it up right away; my editors are screaming at me," the publisher continues.

"Mellow out, man, your negative energy is not helping matters at all." The software man looks around the room. "I sense a lot of tension around here. I think you ought to have a group."

"A group?"

"Yes, I think you need some let-it-all-hang-out group interaction. Look, I'm really sorry but I must take the computer down for a couple of hours. Why don't you order out a couple of pizzas and wine coolers and get some dialogue going with your staff?"

"But, what about the computer?"

"No problem. Programming is like poetry. Energy flows through the bytes and chips... man, I get goosebumps just thinking about it. You have to approach computers existentially. I mean, it's a beautiful thing, man..."

"Just fix the darn thing," the publisher says with a hint of irritation.

"Uh, do you mind if I set up my boom box in the computer room? I find that listening to Mozart tapes helps me tune into the computer. Music soothes the savage computer," he says with a giggle as he disappears into the computer room.

Computer czar shows no mercy

Just as there are outside experts to help computer users, there are in house technicians. These hardy and brave souls are called upon day or night by frantic bosses to fix "little problems."

Here's a report I once wrote on one such technician...

Every so often the newsroom computer at the Daily Herald nears its capacity for storing data.

When that happens the great purges begin.

They come soon after the warning lights on the computer's mainframe begin flashing and the computer begins spewing out printouts saying if something isn't done soon, the system will suffer a fatal crash.

This cry for help seems to trigger a strange metamorphosis within the Herald's normally mild-mannered head computer technician.

A thick mustache and beard suddenly covers his face. And, his quiet midwestern voice gradually becomes deeper and more Slavic sounding. Strangest of all, he begins calling himself The Comp Czar and he starts chanting...

"Purge...purge...purge, your stories must die so the computer can live."

When reporters and editors hear his strange rantings coming from the computer room, they shudder and their faces become twisted expressions of anxiety and fear.

Soon news stories mysteriously disappear from the computer system.

The chanting by the head computer technician becomes louder and more fanatical

Editorials, Ann Landers columns, and sports scores vanish into some irretrievable electronic exile.

Editors rush to the computer room to beg for mercy. They plead with him not to banish Mike Royko or the daily horoscope.

But, he just laughs and turns his thumbs down.

"My baby! My baby! He's got my baby," a reporter yells as she runs through the newsroom after learning her indepth portrait of a Bevent school janitor has disappeared from her computer file.

She falls sobbing at the city editor's feet, but he can only shake his head sympathetically. For he knows he is powerless against the Comp Czar.

No one can stop the purge: Not the chief editor, the publisher or the knights of the Gannett roundtable.

During the Great Purge of 1982, one young and reckless reporter challenged the Comp Czar.

Armed with a copy pencil and a bottle of rubber cement, he raced toward the computer room intent on doing-in the mad technician.

He was just about to deliver a fatal blow, when the Comp Czar pointed to something on his computer terminal screen. It was the reporter's 14-part, eight-month investigative report on city government.

"You wouldn't!" the reporter dared.

The Comp Czar smiled wickedly, hit a button and watched 120,000 words perish into oblivion. His ego mortally wounded, the reporter fell to his knees and began crying uncontrollably.

Editors have been known to offer themselves to the Comp Czar in exchange for sparing their stories. They charm him in every conceivable way and he takes advantage of their every advance.

During one great purge, the entire newsroom staff rose up and stormed the computer room in violent show of force.

They were about to stone the Comp Czar with Webster's Collegiate dictionaries, when he turned to his computer terminal and began killing stories at a furious pace. Suddenly editors and reporters broke ranks and rushed back to their own terminals in desperate hopes of hiding their stories before the Czar got to them.

A river of journalistic blood was spilled in that doomed coup d'etat.

The purges end as quickly as they begin. When the warning lights stop flashing, the Comp Czar turns back into being a mild-mannered technician.

But, every so often he gets that evil gleam in his eyes and under his breath can be heard..."purge...purge ....PURGE!"

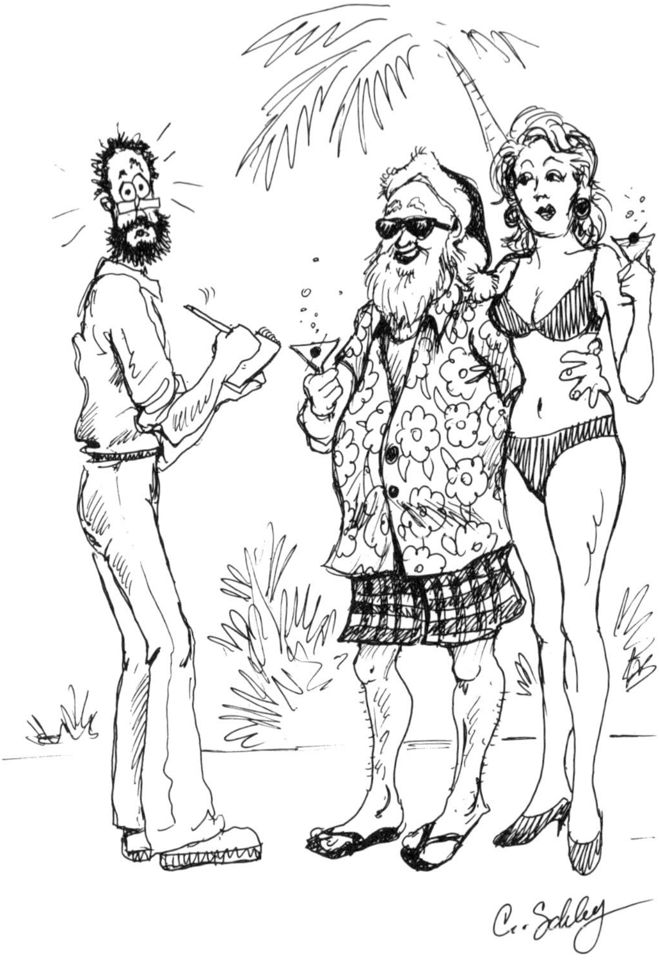

Chapter Eight

The saga of Santa in L.A.

This is the story of the year Santa decided to move his operation south...

The Wildwoods is about to scoop the world press, so pay attention because the last time we scooped anybody dinosaurs still walked the Earth.

Santa Claus lives in Los Angeles, Calif.

Following up on a tip from an inebriated elf in a Burbank bar, I gave ol' St. Nick a call...

"Hello?" says a deep and sexy female voice.

"Mr. Claus please."

"Uh, he's not here..."

"Is this Mrs. Claus?"

There's a long pause.

"This is Raquel, Mr. Claus' personal secretary and rollerskating coach."

"It's urgent I talk with Mr. Claus," I say sternly.

"Well, I think he's out in the Jacuzzi. I'll switch you to the poolside phone."

I hear a few clicks followed by the sound of something falling into water.

"Hello? Hello?" an old man's voice says frantically.

"Hello?" I reply.

"Whew, I thought I drowned ya," the old man chuckles.

"Uh, this is Donald Oakland, a wishing-he-were-there columnist calling from Wausau, Wisconsin.

"Warsaw?" the man replies with a hint of confusion.

"Wausau, you know Wausau Insurance Companies, 60 Minutes..."

"Oh."

"Santa, what the heck are you doing in L.A.?"

"Silicon chips. They make 'em out here."

"What do silicon chips have to do with Christmas?"

"What do you think runs all those video games? Marshmallows?" Santa replies with some irritation.

"Well, uh."

"Every kid and his grandmother is asking for video games this Christmas. The only way I can meet the demand is to set up a plant in Silicon Valley.

"Used to be you could make a kid happy giving him a red fire truck. Now they aren't smiling unless they're shooting down spaceships or chasing rat-mans..."

"That's Pac-Man, Santa."

"Whatever. Anyway, years ago I got real cute handwritten Christmas lists. Now I get computer printouts.

"Just the other day, I got a letter from a kid asking for a 40 megabyte microprocessor for his home computer. Cripes, I've got five elves going to MIT just to decipher these things!"

"I see."

"But, that's not the worst of it," Santa says with a sigh. "I'm having an awfully hard time keeping my elves on the job."

"What, can't handle the smog?"

"Smog is the least of my worries. My third shift foreman didn't show up yesterday. Turns out he was sunbathing all day with some long-legged actress who thought he was Dudley Moore."

"I guess Hollywood has a few more distractions than the North Pole," I reply sympathetically.

"The other day Hugh Hefner threw a bash for my little guys. Only half showed up for work the next morning! Let me tell you, a hungover elf is an ugly sight."

"Well, at least the other half..."

"The other half we haven't found yet," he snaps back.

"They tell me one of the guys is in Spain filming a movie with Roman Polanski and a couple more were picked up at the Dubuque Municipal Airport trying to sell Playboy key cards to Iowa corn farmers!" he yells into the phone.

"Uh, other than that, how are you finding sunny California," I say trying to change the subject and get the old codger in a better mood.

"I tell you, if it weren't for this hot tub and some vitamin fruit drink Raquel whips up, I'd be going bonkers...LOOK OUT!"

The sound of a huge splash comes over the phone.

"Crazy elf just hang-glided into my Jacuzzi. RAQUEL! Kindly remove this kamikaze gnome... and bring me my blood pressure pills...Hey, Wildwoods, I gotta go." The phone clicks dead.

A couple of weeks later, I placed another call to the Patron of the Presents.

"Hello, is Santa Claus there?"

"You from the *National Enquirer*?" an old man's voice says meekly.

"No."

There's a deep sigh on the other end.

"This is Santa speaking, what can I do for you?"

"This is Don Oakland, fearless columnist of the Wausau Daily Herald. Remember me?

"Warsaw?"

"WAH SAW! You know Wausau Insurance Companies, 60 minutes... two hours east of the Green Bay Packers!"

"Oh yeah, I remember you. Hey, I don't want to talk to newspapers," he says angrily.

"How come."

"Yesterday I went to the supermarket to pick up some Budweiser and next to the checkout is the *National Enquirer* with "Is Mrs. Claus Giving St. Nick the Slip?" across the top of the page.

"And, underneath is a picture of my wife coming out of Studio 54 arm in arm with Robin Williams."

"Well, Santa I'm sure they're just friends..."

"I tell you, I don't know what's come over that woman. A week after she arrived from the North Pole she joined a Jane Fonda fitness class.

"The next thing I know, she's spending all her time on Rodeo Drive buying high-priced designer clothes. I mean, up north she looked fine in a red suit and black boots. Now she won't leave the house without her Halston coat.

"And, I read a cover story about her in *People* magazine which hints that she's dating the likes of Roger Moore and Warren Beatty at popular Palm Springs night spots."

"Well, Mr. Claus," I say gently. "I'm sure after spending umpteen years in the North Pole she's entitled to a little fun."

"Oh, I suppose. But, my elves! I tell Santa's little helpers to get their rears in gear and they reply 'Oh wow' or ' Grody to the max.'

"And, I think they're conspiring against me..."

"Come on, Santa."

"I'm not kidding. There's a rumor that those munchkins have created a video game called Shoot Down Santa.

"Across the top of the screen slides an image of myself and my reindeer. The player presses buttons to fire missiles at me... 10 points for each reindeer hit, 25 points for hitting Rudolph and 50 points for hitting me!"

"By the way, how is ol' Rudolph?" I ask, trying to change to a lighter topic.

A loud groan comes over the line.

"A couple of days ago, Rudolph was grazing and got to chewing some green-colored weed. A few hours later, the LAPD calls and says Rudolph was found trying to break into a posh Bel Aire riding stable.

"I mean, he thinks he's a horse. He wants no part of pulling a sled, says it's degrading. Anyway, he says, horses can't fly.

"We've got him in an intensive detox center in Beverly Hills. I have great hopes this guru veterinarian can pull him out of it."

"How are you holding up, Santa?"

"Well, I think I'll live through Christmas. Afterwards I'll either head north for 11 months of well deserved rest or I may start a winery in Napa Valley.

"I mean, if Orson Wells can hawk Paul Masson, why can't I sell Santa Claus Chablis.

"Hey, Wildwoods, I've got to go. Johnny Carson has asked me to come on his show. My writers and I have to come up with a few jokes. How this one sound...

"I tried to fill Presiden Reagan's Christmas wish, but I couldn't stuff all of Congress in my sack. Ha Ha Ha!"

"Bye, Santa," I groaned as I hung up.

Several weeks later I received an invitation to attend Santa's pre-Christmas bash. I mortgaged my car and flew west to witness Santa's last hurrah before making his Christmas rounds.

A servant ushered me through the two-story Tudor style mansion and into a backyard that looked like the back nine of Pebble Beach Country Club.

And, people! It seemed like all of Hollywood was there.

There was Larry "JR" Hagman trying to cheat Patrick Duffey out his Christmas presents.

And, Mick Jagger sat picking "The First Noel" on his electric guitar as Willie Nelson hummed along.

A big crowd gathered around the pool to watch E.T. do a one-and-a-half gainer off the high dive.

My star gazing daze ended abruptly when I felt a light tap on my shoulder. I turned around to find a long-legged gal who looked a lot like Vanna White. She was wearing a tiny red bikini with white fur trim and black boots. On her head was a set of plastic reindeer horns.

"Would you care for a drink?" she said with a husky voice.

"Uh, sure," I stuttered. I took a glass of white wine off her silver tray.

"Merry Christmas," she whispered and kissed my cheek. I felt my knees beginning to buckle.

"Hey Wildwoods!" I looked up and saw Santa rolling down the garden path on skates. Flanking him were two gals who looked like Loni Anderson and Bo Derek.

Santa wore a flower print shirt open to the belly. On his chest was a big gold chain. He had a racquetball racquet in one hand and a Margarita in the other.

"How'd you know it was me?" I asked as he rolled up.

"Hey, babe, you've got Wisconsin drab written all over you. Loosen up, man," he said with a broad smile.

"I just want your readers to know the North Pole is nowhere. Up there it's icicles and polar bears, but down here it's...." He turned and smiled at the gal who looked like Bo Derek.

"Even Ms Claus loves it," he said pointing to his wife who was helping Jane Fonda lead an aerobics class.

A bell atop the mansion rang.

Suddenly the "Theme from Rocky" blared from loudspeakers throughout the backyard. A film crew headed by Francis Ford Coppola popped out from behind a hedge and turned camera and lights toward Santa.

"Let's do it!" Santa yelled. Immediately two burly men lifted him off the ground as two elves pulled off his roller skates. The men then dropped him into his red and white snow suit and black boots.

Santa gulped down the last of his drink and started walking quickly toward the big red sleigh parked by the pool.

A group of elves quickly hitched up the reindeer. At the head of the team was Rudolph. Around his neck dangled a "Don't Nuke Reindeer" medallion.

Santa stood in the sleigh barking out pre-flight checks to his elves. When one elf gave a thumbs up sign, Santa dropped a pair of aviator sunglasses in front of his eyes, grabbed the reins and cried out: "OK Rudy, it's showtime!"

In a moment the sleigh was high above the mansion. As all eyes turned skyward, Santa's voice floated down...

"Faaaar Outtttt!"

Christmas went off without a hitch that year. However, we learned some unsettling news a few days later.

Santa Claus had been kidnapped as he got off his sleigh at his exclusive Beverly Hills mansion.

Witnesses said he was grabbed by three men wearing gray flannel suits and whisked away in a black limo.

After an extensive investigation, I was able to locate a source close to the kidnapping. We shall call Tinsel Throat in order to protect his identity.

Here's his account of the incident...

"Mr. Tinsel Throat, is Santa alive and well?" I asked.

"Oh, he's fine. He's being detained at a secret chalet deep in the North Pole."

"Why?"

"Santa and Mrs. Claus are being deprogrammed. We are weaning them from the corrupt influence of the Southern California lifestyle. In other words, we are trying to cure him the the Hollywood syndrome.

"We?"

"We are members of a multi-national corporation which owns and operates Christmas."

"Huh??"

"Years ago Santa realized he could no longer handle Christmas by himself. Because of the burgeoning material wealth, rising standards of living and rampant greed in the world, it was becoming impossible to deliver all the presents on Christmas Eve.

"In a secret deal, we agreed to purchase his operation with the understanding he would continue his correspondence with children and make Christmas deliveries.

"We would handle the bookkeeping, inventory control, purchasing, personnel management, contract negotiations, etc."

"So, Santa is merely a figurehead?"

"Wrong. Santa is our worldwide representative of Christmas. He is Christmas and must always remain such. We just handle the behind-the-scenes stuff."

"So why kidnap him?" I asked.

"Santa's move to L.A. from a corporate standpoint was wise. It placed our production facilities closer to the source of computer components needed for all those video and computer games people are asking for.

"However, we didn't realize how vulnerable Santa was to the corrupting lifestyle of Hollywood types.

"The wild parties... Santa's name splashed across scandal sheets... the decadence surrounding him was threatening the public's perception of Santa."

"So, you'll lock him away at the North Pole for the rest of his days?" I asked.

"Away from the influences of Hollywood, Santa will soon regain his sensibilities and again realize the responsibilities of his position.

"You see, the spirit of Christmas is so very fragile. Santa personifies that spirit and strengthens it.

"So long as Santa exists, the true spirit of Christmas, the sharing and expressions of love for all humanity, will live on. And, there will always be that Christmas gleam in the eyes of children around the globe.

"Needless to say, a gray bearded old man parading about in a jogging suit, drinking Margaritas and telling jokes on Johnny Carson's show doesn't do much for the children or the spirit of Christmas."

"You have a point there," I said.

"Neither does his playing tag with a 747 over Chicago Christmas night or buzzing the White House at three in the morning."

"So, next year we will have our Santa back?"

"Not only back, but better," Tinsel Throat said with a smile. The Beverly Hills experience will undoubtedly strengthen his resolve to show children and adults there's more to Christmas than accumulating more toys.

Unfortunately, I doubt if we'll be able to cure his penchant for Margaritas," the little man said with a long sigh.

The following Christmas I again tracked down Santa to see if indeed the little man had succeeded in his mission...

'Twas the night before Christmas.. and...Santa was sitting in front of his IBM- XT.

"Ah, Mr. Claus, shouldn't you be getting ready to make your Christmas deliveries," I asked as I entered his North Pole workshop.

"And, shouldn't you be dressed in your bright red outfit instead of a gray three-piece suit?"

The only hint of Christmas on Santa was a tie tack that resembled a holly wreath. It read : "Xmas '85--Be There."

"No need to get ready, boy," Santa said with a casual smile. "I'm not going anywhere tonight."

"What! If you don't deliver all those presents...why millions of children will be heartsick Christmas morning," I protested.

"Oh, they'll get their presents all right. But, instead of sleigh deliver, I'm having Federal Express do it," the old man said.

"Huh?"

"Sure, why not let the professionals handle it. This year I'm contracting with Federal Express, UPS, Emery... the whole overnight air express industry...to deliver Christmas presents this year."

"You getting lazy in your old age, Santa?"

"Nah, I just have better things to do. With the sophistication and reliability of air express today, I'm sure the presents will get there just as fast, although I chuckle when I picture a UPS man crawling down a chimney.

"And, it's less expensive," Santa added.

"Come on, less expensive than delivery by sleigh. Heck, with a sleigh you don't even have fuel costs," I said incredulously.

The old fellow leaned back and laughed.

225

"You have any idea how much it costs to feed a team of reindeer today? Let me tell you, those critters won't pull a sleigh on an empty stomach. Why, they burn so many calories on a Christmas run, I have to stop every two hours to feed them.

"And, going out into that night air is no picnic. Why, last year I was off work for two weeks because of a nasty cold. And, two Christmases ago, Rudolph darn near died of pneumonia," Santa said in a serious voice.

"Every year it seems like at least two reindeer pull a muscle. Let me tell you, at 30 below, you aren't very limber.

"So this year I said, 'Santa, you're getting too old for this nonsense, let the professionals handle it.'

"Anyway, it would give me more time for my business."

"Business?" I asked.

Santa turned to his computer and hit a couple of keys. Onto the screen flashed stock, currency and commodity prices from around the world.

For several minutes, Santa forgot about his visitor and began placing phone calls to brokers in New York, London and Toyko.

"Uh, Santa?" I interrupted.

Santa shut off the computer and turned to me. "Christmas is only a small part of what I do. The rest of the year I run Santa Enterprises, a multi-national investment conglomerate.

"You see, over the years I have invested in companies world-wide, companies which have products or services related to the toy industry. Since Santa knows who's been naughty or nice, I have a slight advantage in, shall we say, selecting growth stocks," he said with a smirk.

Suddenly a red phone rang.

"Yeah?" Santa growled. It was his chief elf on the other end. "Whadaya mean, UPS blew a jet engine in Nashville; Federal Express is grounded by fog at Heathrow and everything west of Dubuque is snowed in. You say there is a strike in Italy and all my presents are still sitting on the docks!"

Santa slammed down the receiver. "Well, as they say, the best laid plans..."

Santa flicked on an intercom.

"Rudoph! Assemble the troops...On Dancer, on Prancer, on Donner and Vixen!"

He turned to me again as elves ran frantically around the room getting his gear together.

"Alas, if you want something done right, you have to do it yourself," he said as he ran out of the room toward his sleigh.

The following Christmas, I again checked in on Santa. I was curious if he had developed an ulcer. What I found was quite the opposite.

"Hello? Is Santa there?"

There was a long silence.

"This is the North Pole isn't it?"

"Yeah," said a gruff voice, "but Santa isn't around."

"He's not in California again?" I asked.

"Nah, he's out cross country skiing."

"Skiing?"

"Yeah, weird ain't it? It's 40 below up here, we're eight days behind in toy production and he's out doing a quick 20 K."

"Well, a little physical exercise never hurt anyone," I countered.

"Little! Nothing ol' wide belly does is ever little. I tell you, he's driving us crazy! For years we went about building toys and answering Santa's mail. Now every morning we have to exercise to Richard Simmons on the TV.

"This isn't Santa's workshop anymore. It's Camp Lejeune!"

"How come Santa's into fitness?" I asked.

"It's the fault of his business manager. This hot shot elf in a three-piece suit flew up from New York last spring and told Santa that if he didn't shape up, his health insurance and workman's comp premiums would fly higher than his sleigh on Christmas Eve.

"He told Santa that given his rotund condition and the fact he lugged around large sacks all day, crawled down chimneys and rode in open sleighs without a seat belt, that he, Santa, was a prime candidate for a massive comp claim."

The elf's voice became more exasperated. "The next day Santa goes off and buys exercise books and a sweatsuit. Next thing we know, he's hooked on his health and ours, too!"

A long pause followed.

"The wife is just as bad!" the elf said in a hushed voice.

"Mrs. Claus," the voice paused for a moment. "Thinks she's Linda Evans!

"All day she jumps around in front of the VCR that is playing a Jane Fonda videotape.

"Don't get me wrong, Mrs. Claus is a nice looking lady, but she's built like a basketball.

"It's quite a sight to see this grandmother-type in hot pink leotards, her bulges bouncing to the beat of Mick Jagger. All I can say is it's an awesome sight," he said, beginning to laugh.

"Oh, oh, Santa's coming. I'll put him on, but not a word about our little conversation."

"Claus here." There was the sound of heavy puffing on the other end.

"This is Wildwoods, Santa. How's life treating you?"

"Super! Just finished 15 K, burned the wax right off my Rossignols," he said with a hearty laugh. "I tell you, Wildwoods, a little Vitamin E and prune juice and you'll feel 20 years younger," he said enthusiastically.

"Last Christmas I was pushing 275. This summer I shed 30 pounds and by Christmas I'm going to hit 190. No more roly-poly, jolly ol' Saint Nick this year, by golly!

"Heck, I'm not even going to wear my red suit this Christmas. I've got this University of Wisconsin sweatsuit and Bucky Badger stocking cap that will do just fine."

"But, tradition!" I protested.

"Heck with tradition. Hey, you tell your readers, Santa's tougher than Mr. T! You'd better be good and you'd better be fit, if you expect anything from me!" he said loudly.

"Gotta go now, my Nautilus machine beckons." he said just before hanging up.